BOOKS BY MARGARET MEAD

COMING OF AGE IN SAMOA

GROWING UP IN NEW GUINEA

THE CHANGING CULTURE OF AN INDIAN TRIBE

SEX AND TEMPERAMENT IN THREE PRIMITIVE SOCIETIES

FROM THE SOUTH SEAS

AND KEEP YOUR POWDER DRY

BALINESE CHARACTER: A PHOTOGRAPHIC ANALYSIS *with Gregory Bateson*

MALE AND FEMALE

GROWTH AND CULTURE: A PHOTOGRAPHIC STUDY OF BALINESE CHILDHOOD *with Frances C. Macgregor*

THE SCHOOL IN AMERICAN CULTURE

SOVIET ATTITUDES TOWARD AUTHORITY

NEW LIVES FOR OLD: CULTURAL TRANSFORMATION—MANUS, 1928–1953

AN ANTHROPOLOGIST AT WORK: WRITINGS OF RUTH BENEDICT

PEOPLE AND PLACES

CONTINUITIES IN CULTURAL EVOLUTION

ANTHROPOLOGY: A HUMAN SCIENCE

ANTHROPOLOGISTS AND WHAT THEY DO

FAMILY *with Kenneth Heyman*

THE WAGON AND THE STAR: A STUDY OF AMERICAN COMMUNITY INITIATIVE *with Muriel Brown*

THE SMALL CONFERENCE: AN INNOVATION IN COMMUNICATION *with Paul Byers*

BOOKS EDITED BY MARGARET MEAD

COOPERATION AND COMPETITION AMONG PRIMITIVE PEOPLES

CULTURAL PATTERNS AND TECHNOLOGICAL CHANGE

PRIMITIVE HERITAGE: AN ANTHROPOLOGICAL ANTHOLOGY *with Nicholas Calas*

THE STUDY OF CULTURE AT A DISTANCE *with Rhoda Metraux*

CHILDHOOD IN CONTEMPORARY CULTURES *with Martha Wolfenstein*

THE GOLDEN AGE OF AMERICAN ANTHROPOLOGY *with Ruth Bunzel*

AMERICAN WOMEN *with Frances B. Kaplan*

SCIENCE AND THE CONCEPT OF RACE *with Theodosius Dobzhansky and Ethel Tobach*

Since 1925, when she began her pioneering field work with primitive peoples of the South Pacific, Margaret Mead has been uninterruptedly involved in the study of man's cultural evolution.

Born in Philadelphia in 1901, Margaret Mead was educated at Barnard College and Columbia University. At the age of twenty-three, after completing her graduate work in anthropology, she spent nine months living with and studying the isolated inhabitants of American Samoa. Her research resulted in the classic *Coming of Age in Samoa*, originally published in 1928. In 1926 she became a member of the staff of The American Museum of Natural History, and began a long series of studies of different parts of the Pacific—to fill out her knowledge of the Pacific cultures which were her responsibility at the Museum—and to enlarge our knowledge of different aspects of human life. She had studied adolescence in Samoa; in 1928–29 she studied early childhood among the Manus, followed by studies of male and female differences and infant development in other New Guinea tribes. Her findings were published in *Sex and Temperament in Three Primitive Societies* in 1936 and *Male and Female* in 1949. She did similar studies in Bali from 1936–39.

After the birth of her daughter in 1939, Margaret Mead devoted the next ten years to the application of anthropological insights, first to wartime problems, and later to the exploration of contemporary cultures. In 1953 she returned to Manus, to record the dramatic postwar progress of the community she had studied in 1928, described in *New Lives for Old*. In 1965 and 1966 she made further short trips to Manus and in 1967 she participated in the filming of a ninety-minute color sound film for National Educational Television, *Margaret Mead's New Guinea Journal*—showing the gigantic strides into the modern world of a people whom she had known as stone-age children.

For her tireless and imaginative pursuit of knowledge about human potentialities, Margaret Mead has won world-wide recognition both from her colleagues and from the general public. The recipient of many honorary degrees and awards, she was named Outstanding Woman of the Year in the Field of Science by the Associated Press

(1949) and One of the Outstanding Women of the Twentieth Century by Nationwide Women Editors (1965). She has been president of the American Anthropological Association (1960), the World Federation for Mental Health (1956–57), and is currently president of the World Society for Ekistics. She has been a trustee of Hampton Institute in Virginia since 1945.

In June 1969 Margaret Mead became Curator Emeritus of Ethnology of The American Museum of Natural History. She has continued her teaching as adjunct Professor of Anthropology at Columbia University and Visiting Professor of Anthropology in the Department of Psychiatry at the University of Cincinnati's Medical College. She is also Chairman of the Division of Social Sciences at Fordham's new Liberal Arts College at Lincoln Center. In addition to her own books and monographs, Dr. Mead has coauthored many books with younger collaborators and writes a monthly column for *Redbook Magazine*.

In her field work, Margaret Mead has been able to follow the children she studied into their adulthood in Manus, Bali, and New Guinea, and in her own lifetime, she, as the granddaughter, daughter, and mother of professional women, has participated actively in our rapidly changing world.

CULTURE AND COMMITMENT

MARGARET MEAD

CULTURE
AND COMMITMENT

A STUDY OF THE GENERATION GAP

Published for

THE AMERICAN MUSEUM OF NATURAL HISTORY

Natural History Press/Doubleday & Company, Inc.

Garden City, New York/1970

The Natural History Press, publisher for The American Museum of Natural History, is a division of Doubleday & Company, Inc. Directed by a joint editorial board made up of members of the staff of both the Museum and Doubleday, the Natural History Press publishes books and periodicals in all branches of the life and earth sciences, including anthropology and astronomy. The Natural History Press has its editorial offices at The American Museum of Natural History, Central Park West at 79th Street, New York, New York 10024, and its business offices at 501 Franklin Avenue, Garden City, New York 11530.

This book originated from the *Man and Nature* lectures delivered by Margaret Mead at The American Museum of Natural History in March 1969 in conjunction with the Museum's centennial celebration.

Grateful acknowledgment is made to the National Institute of Mental Health, Research Grant MH–3303–01 1961–1965, "The Factor of Mental Health in Allopsychic Orientation."

To
My father's mother
and
My daughter's daughter

PREFACE

Twenty years ago, as we prepared for the White House Conference on Children, the central problem agitating young people and those who were concerned with them was identity. In the midst of the tremendous changes going on in the world in the period immediately following World War II it was clear that it was becoming harder and harder for any individual then growing up to find his or her place within the conflicting versions of our culture and within the world that was already pressing in upon us through television, even though the world-wide sharing of national tragedy and cosmic adventure was yet to come.

Today, the central problem is commitment: to what past, present, or future can the idealistic young commit themselves? Commitment in this sense would have been a meaningless question to primitive preliterate man. He was what he was: one of his own people, a people who very often used a special name for human beings to describe their own in contrast to all others. He might fail; he might be ejected from his group; he might under extreme circumstances elect to flee; he might, deprived of his land, become a slave on the land of another people; he might in some parts of the world commit suicide out of personal despair or anger. But he could not change his commitment. He was who he was—inalienable, sheltered and fed within the cocoon of custom until his whole being expressed it.

The idea of choice in commitment entered human history when competing styles of life were endowed with new kinds of sanction of religious or political ideology. No longer a matter of minor comparisons between tribes, as civilization developed commitment became a matter of choice between entire systems of thought. In the phrasings of Middle Eastern religions, one system became right, all others wrong; in the gentler words of Asian religions, other systems "provided a different way." It was then that the question: *To which do I commit*

my life? was raised for the thoughtful in a form that only temporarily disappears when faith and society and culture are temporarily reunited in isolated and barricaded forms in closed
religious sects like the Hutterites—or behind iron curtains into
which no alien note is permitted to enter.

In this century, with rising insistence and anguish, there is
now a new note: *Can I commit my life to anything? Is there
anything in human cultures as they exist today worth saving,
worth committing myself to?* We find the suicide of the fortunate and the gifted, the individual who feels no abiding and
unquestioning tie with any social form. Just as man is newly
faced with the responsibility for not destroying the human race
and all living things and for using his accumulated knowledge
to build a safe world, so at this moment the individual is freed
to stand aside and question, not only his belief in God, his belief in science, or his belief in socialism, but his belief in anything at all.

It is my conviction that in addition to the world conditions
that have given rise to this search for new commitment and
to this possibility of no commitment at all, we also have new
resources for facing our situation, new grounds for commitment. It is to this theme that this book is addressed. It is written in the belief that only as we come to terms with our past
and our present is there a future for the oldest and the young-
est among us who share the total round.

February 21, 1969

The American Museum of Natural History
New York City
The United States of America

CONTENTS

INTRODUCTION

An essential and extraordinary aspect of man's present state is that, at this moment in which we are approaching a world-wide culture and the possibility of becoming fully aware citizens of the world in the late twentieth century, we have simultaneously available to us for the first time examples of the ways men have lived at every period over the last fifty thousand years: primitive hunters and fishermen; people who have only digging sticks to cultivate their meager crops; people living in cities that are still ruled in theocratic and monarchical style; peasants who live as they have lived for a thousand years, encapsulated and walled off from urban cultures; peoples who have lost their ancient and complex cultures to take up simple, crude, proletarian existences in the new; and peoples who have left thousands of years of one kind of culture to enter the modern world, with none of the intervening steps. At the time that a New Guinea native looks at a pile of yams and pronounces them "a lot" because he cannot count them, teams at Cape Kennedy calculate the precise second when an Apollo mission must change its course if it is to orbit around the moon. In Japan, sons in the thirteenth generation of potters who make a special ceremonial pot are still forbidden to touch a potter's wheel or work on other forms of pottery. In some places old women search for herbs and mutter spells to relieve the fears of pregnant girls, while elsewhere research laboratories outline the stages in reproductivity that must each be explored for better contraceptives. Armies of twenty savage men go into the field to take one more victim from a people they have fought for five hundred years, and international assemblies soberly assay the vast destructiveness of nuclear weapons. Some fifty thousand years of our history lie spread out before us, accessible, for this brief moment in time, to our simultaneous inspection.

This is a situation that has never occurred before in human

history and, by its very nature, can never occur in this way again. It is because the entire planet is accessible to us that we can know that there are no people anywhere about whom we might know but do not. One mystery has been resolved for us forever as it applies to earth, and future explorations must take place among the planets and the stars. We have the means of reaching all of earth's diverse peoples and we have the concepts that make it possible for us to understand them, and they now share in a world-wide, technologically propagated culture, within which they are able to listen as well as to talk to us. For the one-sided explorations of the early anthropologist who recorded the strange kinship systems of alien peoples, to whom he himself was utterly unintelligible, we now can substitute open-ended conversations, conducted under shared skies, when airplanes fly over the most remote mountains, and primitive people can tune in transistor radios or operate tape recorders in the most remote parts of the world. The past culture of complex civilizations is largely inaccessible to the technologically simplest peoples of the world. They know nothing of three thousand years of Chinese civilization, or of the great civilizations of the Middle East, or of the tradition of Greece and Rome from which modern science has grown. The step from their past to our present is condensed, but they share one world with us, and their desire for all that new technology and new forms of organization can bring, now serves as a common basis for communication.

This has happened while many other things have been happening in the world. The old colonial empires have broken up. Countries with a dozen college graduates have become nations, and peoples newly joined together politically demand to be heard as nations. The voiceless and the oppressed in every part of the world have begun to demand more power. Fourth-grade children conduct sit-ins and undergraduates claim the right to choose their professors. A profound disturbance is occurring in the relationships between the strong and the weak, the possessors and the dispossessed, elder and younger, and those who have knowledge and skill and those who lack them. The secure belief that those who knew had authority over those who did not has been shaken.

Profound as these changes are, I do not think we would have found it easy to bring into our councils the full contribution of members of exotic and primitive cultures, if at the same time a world-wide culture had not been developing.

In 1967, after an absence of twenty-nine years, I returned to the village of Tambunam on the Sepik River in New Guinea. In many ways progress had passed it by. Although the mission had been admitted to the village to provide schooling for children, ceremonies had been constricted, war abolished, and the great men's house removed, these people still built their beautiful dwelling houses, worked sago, and fished as they had always done. Yet there was a difference. In the 1930s, when one arrived in a New Guinea village, the first requests were for medicine, as someone came forward with a festering wound or bad laceration, and for trade goods—razor blades, fishhooks, salt, adze blades, cloth. The European was expected to bring material objects from the outside world and, if he stayed, to make it easier for the village people to obtain these goods. But in 1967, the first question was:

Have you got a tape recorder?

Yes, why?

We have heard other people's singing on the radio and we want other people to hear ours.

A major shift. Through the spread of a world culture of transistor radios and democratic theories about the value of each small culture, the people of Tambunam had heard New Guinea music, which it was now government policy to broadcast, and they had come to feel that they could participate, on an equal footing, in this new world of broadcasting. This was not all. As my colleague, Rhoda Metraux, began to record their music, they became skilled critics and producers, learning how to hear the interfering sounds of dogs barking and babies crying— sounds they had never attended to when there was no tape recorder to tell them how much of the repertoire of village sounds was audible and how these sounds spoiled their performance. As they listened to the nondiscriminating, pedantic tape, a new set of self-perceptions was available to them. They now included the direction of the wind as they considered how their music could be recorded best and they learned to modulate the loudness of percussion instruments to match the carrying quality of different singers' voices. The kind of awareness that is the first step in an ability to participate in social science had reached them through a new climate of opinion and a new technology. They shared our world and could contribute to it in a new way.

Are we to face a new situation, confronted simultaneously by what is happening all over the world? For today we can visit a Shriners' hospital for burned children and find there the extraordinary beauty and devotion of a whole team of highly trained doctors and nurses who dedicate thousands of hours to the care of a badly burned child, patiently regrafting skin and remodeling features to give to a brave and optimistic child a semblance of what he might have been. Such single-minded devotion to recovery, to remade skin, and to simulated hands, gives one an extraordinary hope for the future. We see, however, that in that same hospital another child who has no capacity for such optimism and who faces with despair his future as a deformed and mutilated creature is still forced to live, ingenuously and lovingly wooed back to life and partial functioning by the same system that saves his optimistic little roommate. When we realize that those who have given money and time and skill to make such miracles possible are citizens, and in most cases not actively dissenting citizens, of a country engaged each day in a war in which more children are burned with napalm than such hospitals save in a year, one's heart falters. Are we trapped, one is forced to ask? Are we trapped, not by a set of immutable instincts which determine that we will always in all cases turn to aggression and exploitation of others whenever we are strong enough—or, to quote an equally persuasive theory, whenever we are too weak? But are we trapped instead within a set of inventions called civilization that is now so well supported by technology and population expansion that we must follow a predetermined course to destruction, just as all the earlier civilizations did, but this time on a planetary scale which will end the history of the inhabitants of Terra of Sol?

If I believed that this were so, that the greater man's capacity to invent, elaborate, and transmit complex cultures, the more surely he would be trapped in a cultural setting which, while it permitted great achievements, would ultimately lead to destruction and horror, I should not have given these lectures. The role of Cassandra is a useful one only if it is not believed by the prophets themselves. Who will take the trouble to warn of the doom to come unless some preferred future alternative is offered, either in steps that will avert that doom or in preparation for a next world? As doomsday is preached more vigorously, the more one is committed to a better world. It may be the spurious promise that man, having ravished and destroyed earth, will set off for another planet. Or it may be the completely transcendental alternative that the Lord has had enough of us and will allow us to precipitate catastrophes that will permit the chosen to enter heaven and the rejected to burn forever in the fires of hell.

When the causes of great catastrophes were not understood, a conception of a God who purified with fire or flood, but saved some men for a future of earth, was a tenable one, a belief in fact that permitted those who held it to survive through the most terrible vicissitudes. It permitted men to live and pit their strength and optimism against tremendous odds, confident that they, the chosen people, would survive. So men have returned to build again and again on the slopes of volcanoes; in Kansas the residents of each small town that has never had a tornado continue to believe that they, favored above others, will never have one. And in some American communities scientists have joined in the protests of local citizens against the location of dangerous facilities near *their* cities, fully conscious that if their protests were successful the missile site would be built near someone else's city. The physicist, Leo Szilard, low in faith in the species of which he was such a distinguished member, proposed a hostage system to prevent nuclear war that would depend on the aggressive self-interest of one American city versus another if cities of a certain size were marked for sacrifice.

None of these partial views of man as sometimes condemned and sometimes chosen, in either secular or religious form, stands up within our present single intercommunicating worldwide settlement pattern. No spurious pattern of promise of escape in space colonization, no doctrine of a God who would destroy the many to save a few, no persistence of blind optimism will suffice. The prophet who fails to present a bearable alternative and yet preaches doom is part of the trap that he postulates. Not only does he picture us caught in a tremendous man-made or God-made trap from which there is no escape, but we also must listen to him day in, day out, describe how the trap is inexorably closing. To such prophecies the human race, as presently bred and educated and situated, is incapable of listening. So some dance and some immolate themselves as human torches; some take drugs and some artists spill their creativity in sets of randomly placed dots on a white ground. The concerned may be too few to take the steps needed to save us. Unless there are enough such men, we are doomed. So I stand here, not as a Cassandra, but as one who lived through the urgencies of World War II when, under pressure of what seemed inevitable disaster, we as a people were able to rally what resources we had to fend off that disaster. And I now believe that one of the essential elements in escape from an infinitely greater threat is the willingness to use—each one of us—what we know now, always acknowledging that what we know is not enough. Then the urgency was great. We foresaw the death of science and humane culture as we had known them, and the submergence of the Western world by a demonic culture that could not only use the technology developed by science, but also prevent science itself from generating liberating humane change. We foresaw a hundred years of "dark ages" and so limited were we, in our conception of time and space, that a hundred years of eclipse of Euro-American culture then seemed too terrible to face. Perhaps it was just because it was thus limited that we could face it. In contrast, the possibility of the disappearance of all human life, of life itself, from this planet is something few human beings can imagine. Using the imagery of theology or science fiction, men see all else destroyed but man himself. Theirs is the same fatuous optimism I myself once displayed as the car in which I was being driven swerved toward what seemed certain destruction. Thinking of the children of the driver soon to be orphaned, I said to myself: "I'll take care of them."

Such optimism is both our hope and our greatest danger. Displayed by a single child, who can testify to our increasing concern for the individual, such optimism may illumine the world. Displayed by members of a whole community, who rebuild their houses on the slopes of an active volcano, it may lead to world-wide destruction. A balance between individual optimism and stubborn group blindness is what we seek. Perhaps one of the ways of achieving this balance is to find those who, drawing on their own individual and group history, have an extra capacity for optimism. We can then provide them with the tools of observation and forecasting that will set them looking for new sites for cities, better than the familiar slope of the active volcano. This is what I hope.

I believe that the reason we can look at all the great civilizations of the past and at the successive stages in the history of our own era as a succession of repetitive traps is that *we do not know enough about them.* It is upon great historic emptinesses —the lives of unknown peoples lived out within high-standing broken walls now in ruins, the songs sung to infants that we cannot reconstruct, and the lives of the unsung poor and dispossessed who left no records at all—that the human imagination can project its fantasies and its despair. In history as in science, the grand design without the detail shakes belief and trust to the core. The first understanding of Darwinian theory aroused only anguish in those who trusted their God, and justified a dog-eat-dog social theory in those who did not.

Every detailed exploration of the mechanisms of survival—

of the delicate adjustments that permit many brightly colored creatures to live crowded together in distinctive niches in the tropical seas, and less specialized creatures to move from one habitat to another—modulates the original response of the sensitive to the idea of the survival of the fittest. For the theory of a death instinct in lemmings or rabbits, we can substitute the delicate responses of their enzyme systems to conditions of overcrowding or shortage of food.

Each view of the world, in a crude overstatement of theory, has led us into one trap after another as we have seen human society as a sanctioned analogue of nature red in tooth and claw, or the universe as a machine that man can learn to control, or man himself as a machine-like mechanism that can soon be manufactured in large replicated quantities. But the next advances in theory, the use of new instruments, and finer methods of observation and analysis have transformed these crude exploitative ideas and the complementary despair that they arouse in the sensitive into new levels of complexity.

The appropriate activity for man is no longer to be phrased in terms of the crude maximization of a single variable or a few variables, where loss is balanced by gain and gain inevitably means loss somewhere in the system. Such maximization models are found where crop yield is promoted at the expense of depleting the soil, or polluting the streams; or, in the socio-economic sphere, when one country's economic progress is seen as inevitably linked to another country's loss. Instead of the model of the single isolated organism or the single cell, we may use a biological model, especially an ecological model based on a complex system of many living creatures in interaction with a single environment. In this model, the gain of one part is the gain of another part of the system. Parasite and host are essential to each other; change comes when the internal balance is disturbed and new adjustments have to be made. The old calculus of gain and loss is replaced by negative entropy in which concentrations of information reverse the trend toward disorganization. This is the path man has to take if he is both to use and to escape from his previous scientific insights. In this way, through the understanding that he acquires of the universe he lives in, man in the universe comes to be exemplar and executant of the highest exercise of negative entropy.

All such changes from crude and inherently pessimistic phrasings and conceptions to those that permit room for innovation, consciousness, and salvation proceed from new and relevant research. The various tools made possible by mathematics, electronics, and technology in general can be used with greater and greater precision to explore events, the scale or composition of which have hitherto been taken for granted or which have been treated as units of the larger system without intrinsic characteristics of their own. Each discovery of a new level of scientific penetration of the nature of the universe which includes man opens up new vistas of hope.

It is in this belief that I shall examine our present knowledge of culture, with its basis in the model derived from primitive society. This model is one that was once very badly needed and still offers tremendous possibilities. But it has been both overextended and underdifferentiated during the last twenty-five years. Today there is almost no resemblance between the concept of culture based on the work of the field anthropologist among existing primitive peoples and the concept based on his work that is used in contemporary scientific thought. From the standpoint of what the psychologist, sociologist, or historian attempts to understand, the model of a primitive culture has lent itself to a kind of extrapolation that is crude, deterministic, and reductionist, whether "culture" is labeled an "intervening variable" (to be written off simply by giving the same psychological tests to Puerto Ricans in San Juan and Puerto Ricans in New York) or is treated as a form of Pavlovian conditioning.

In *Continuities in Cultural Evolution*, written ten years ago, I attempted a refinement of the concept of cultural learning. I explored in some detail different mechanisms of learning that coexist today and can be extrapolated into the remote past before language made possible description at a distance, or script made possible the storage of information over time, or photography and electronic recording made possible the storage of unanalyzed events for future analysis.

In this book, drawing on the same materials, I shall explore living cultures of different degrees of complexity, all existing at the present time, but I shall emphasize essential differences, that is, discontinuities, between primitive, historic, and contemporary post-World War II cultures.

Besides the shift from significant continuities to significant discontinuities, there is one other difference between the discussion in *Continuities in Cultural Evolution* and what I discuss in this book. Here I shall not deal with inferred behavior patterns of early man, but only with such behavior patterns as we have actually been able to observe and record among contemporary living primitive peoples. At present the areas about which we have the crudest understanding provide the groundwork for the most pessimistic and destructive kinds of thinking, and these imperfect attempts to reconstruct the behavior of our forebears in the remote past when they were becoming men are impeding the successful transformation of our outmoded contemporary cultures. Patterns discerned in the recently observed and only partly understood behavior of birds, fish, and primates have been prematurely and crudely applied to man, particularly in postulating behaviors of early man for which at present we have insufficient evidence. As one result, theories about human aggression, like those of Lorenz, and the speculations of a dramatist interpreter like Ardrey, serve to encourage the belief in man's inherent beastliness, while reactions to such interpretations, like those of Ashley Montague, which present man as inherently good, confuse rather than clarify our understanding of man. For this reason, I shall draw only on studies of contemporary cultures *in vivo*, and where I make remarks about the past, they will be labeled as inferential and of a different order.

CULTURE AND COMMITMENT

CULTURE AND COMMERCE

CHAPTER ONE

THE PAST

Postfigurative Cultures and Well-Known Forebears

The distinctions I am making among three different kinds of culture—*postfigurative*, in which children learn primarily from their forebears, *cofigurative*, in which both children and adults learn from their peers, and *prefigurative*, in which adults learn also from their children—are a reflection of the period in which we live. Primitive societies and small religious and ideological enclaves are primarily postfigurative, deriving authority from the past. Great civilizations, which necessarily have developed techniques for incorporating change, characteristically make use of some form of cofigurative learning from peers, playmates, fellow students, and fellow apprentices. We are now entering a period, new in history, in which the young are taking on new authority in their prefigurative apprehension of the still unknown future.

A postfigurative culture is one in which change is so slow and imperceptible that grandparents, holding newborn grandchildren in their arms, cannot conceive of any other future for the children than their own past lives. The past of the adults is the future of each new generation; their lives provide the ground plan. The children's future is shaped in such a way that what has come after childhood for their forebears is what they, too, will experience after they are grown.

Postfigurative cultures, in which the elders cannot conceive of change and so can only convey to their descendants this sense of unchanging continuity, have been, on the basis of present evidence, characteristic of human societies for millennia or up to the beginning of civilization. Without written or monumental records, each change had to be assimilated to the known and carried on in the memory and the movement patterns of the elders of each generation. The child's basic learning was conveyed to him so early, so inarticulately, and so surely, as his elders expressed their sense that this was the way things would be for him because he was the child of their bodies and their spirits, their land and their tradition, particular and specific, that his sense of his own identity and his own destiny were unchallengeable. Only the impact of some violent external event—a natural catastrophe or a conquest—could alter this. Contact with other peoples might not change this sense of timelessness at all; the sense of difference reinforced the sense of one's own particular and ineradicable identity. Even the extreme conditions of forced migration, long voyages with no known or certain destination on uncharted seas and arrival on an uninhabited island, only accentuated this sense of continuity.

It is true that the continuity of all cultures depends on the living presence of at least three generations. The essential characteristic of postfigurative cultures is the assumption, expressed by members of the older generation in their every act, that their way of life (however many changes may, in fact, be embodied in it) is unchanging, eternally the same. In the past, before the present extension of life span, living great-grandparents were very rare and grandparents were few. Those who embodied the longest stretch of the culture, who were the models for those younger than themselves, in whose slightest tone or gesture acceptance of the whole way of life was contained, were few and hale. Their keen eyesight, sturdy limbs, and tireless industry represented physical as well as cultural survival. For such a culture to be perpetuated, the old were needed, not only to guide the group to seldom-sought refuges in time of famine, but also to provide the complete model of what life was. When the end of life is already known—when the song that will be sung at death, the offerings that will be made, the spot of earth where one's bones will rest are already designated—each person, according to age and sex, intelligence and temperament, embodies the whole culture.

In such cultures, every object, in its form and in the way it is handled, accepted, rejected, misused or broken or inappropriately venerated, reinforces the way in which every other object is made and used. Each gesture reinforces, recalls and reflects or provides a mirror image or an echo of each other gesture, of which it is a more complete or less complete version. Each utterance contains forms found in other utterances. Any segment of cultural behavior, when analyzed, will be found to have the same underlying pattern, or the same kind of patterned allowances for the existence of other patterns in that culture. The very simple cultures of peoples who have been isolated from other peoples make the point most sharply. But cultures that are very complex may yet be postfigurative in style, and so may display all the characteristics of other postfigurative cultures: the absence of a realization of change and the successful printing, indelibly, upon each child of the cultural form.

The conditions for change are of course always present implicitly, even in the mere repetition of a traditional procedure. As no man steps in the same river twice, so there is always a possibility that some procedure, some custom, some belief, acceded to a thousand times, will rise into consciousness. This chance increases when the people of one postfigurative culture are in close contact with those of another. Their sense of what indeed constitutes their culture is accentuated.

In 1925 after a hundred years of contact with modern cultures, Samoans talked continually about *Samoa* and *Samoan* custom, rebuking small children as *Samoan* children, combining their remembered Polynesian identity and their sense of the contrast between themselves and the colonizing foreigners. In the 1940s, in Venezuela, within a few miles of the city of Maracaibo, Indians still hunted with bows and arrows, but cooked their food in aluminum pots stolen from Europeans, with whom they had never communicated in any way. And in the 1960s, living as enclaves within a foreign country, European or American occupying troops and their families have looked with equally uncomprehending and unaccepting eyes at the "natives"—Germans, Malays, or Vietnamese—who lived outside their compounds. The experience of contrast may only heighten the sense of the elements of changeless identity of the group to which one belongs.

While postfigurative cultures are characteristically intimately related to their habitat, the habitat need not be a single area where twenty generations have tilled the same soul. Such cultures are found also among nomadic peoples who move twice a year, among groups in diaspora, like the Armenians and the Jews, in Indian castes who live represented by small numbers scattered among villages inhabited by many other castes. They may be found among small groups of aristocrats or among outcastes like the Eta of Japan. People who were once parts of complex societies may forget—in foreign lands—the kinds of dynamic responses to realized change that caused them to emigrate, and in the new place they may huddle together, again asserting their unchanging identity with their forebears.

Adoption into such groups, conversion, initiation, circumcision—none of these is impossible; but all such acts convey absolute commitment and irrevocability conveyed by grandparents to their own grandchildren in postfigurative cultures. Membership, normally achieved by birth and sometimes by election, is a matter of total and unquestioning commitment.

The postfigurative culture depends upon the actual presence of three generations. So the postfigurative culture is peculiarly generational. It depends for continuity upon the expectations of the old, and upon the almost ineradicable imprint of those expectations upon the young. It depends upon the adults being able to see the parents who reared them, as they rear their children in the way they themselves were reared. In such a society there is no room for the invocation of mythical parent figures, who in a changing world are so frequently conjured up to justify parental demands—"My father would never have done this or that or t'other"—cannot be resorted to when a grandfather is sitting there, in comfortable league with his small grandson, while the father himself is the opponent of both, through the discipline that exists between father and

son. The whole system is there; it depends upon no version of
the past which is not also shared by those who have heard that
version since they were born and who therefore experience it
as actuality. The answers to the questions: *Who am I? What
is the nature of my life as a member of my culture; how do I
speak and move, eat and sleep, make love, make a living, become a parent, meet my death?* are experienced as predetermined. It is possible for an individual to fail to be as brave or
as parental, as industrious or as generous, as the dictates which
his grandparents' hands conveyed to him, but in his failure he
is as much a member of his culture as others are in their success. If suicide is a known possibility, a few or many may commit suicide; if it is not, the same self-destructive impulses take
other forms. The combination of universal human drives and
available human defense mechanisms, the processes of recognition and apperception, of recognition and recall, of redintegra-
tion, will be there. But the style in which these are combined
will be overridingly particular and distinctive.

The diverse peoples of the Pacific whom I have been studying for forty years illustrate many kinds of postfigurative cultures. The Mountain Arapesh of New Guinea, as they were
living forty-five years ago, displayed one form. In the sureness
and the certainty with which each act was performed—the way
the large toe was used to pick up something from the ground
or the leaves for the mat were bitten off—each act, each gesture
was adapted to all others in ways that reflect the past, a past
that, however many changes it contained, was itself lost. For
the Arapesh there is no past except the past that has been embodied in the old and, in a younger form, in their children and
their children's children. Change there has been, but it has
been so completely assimilated that differences between earlier
and later acquired customs have vanished in the understanding
and the expectations of the people.

As the Arapesh child was fed, held, bathed, and orna-
mented, myriad inexplicit and inarticulate learnings were conveyed to it by the hands that held it, the voices around it, the
cadences of lullaby and dirge. Within the village and between

villages, as the child was carried over and later walked on expected paths, the slightest disturbance of the surface was an event to be registered in the walking feet. When a new house was built, the response of each person who passed it registered for the carried child that there was something new here, something that had not been here a few days before and yet was in no way startling or surprising. The response was as slight as that of the blind to the different feel of sunlight sifted through trees with different kinds of leaves, yet it was there. The appearance of a stranger in the village was registered with equal precision. Muscles tensed as people ran over in their minds how much food they had on hand to placate the dangerous visitor and the probable whereabouts of the men who were away from the village. When a new baby was being born, over the edge of the cliff, in the "evil place" where menstruating and parturient women were sent, the place of defecation and birth, a thousand small familiar signs proclaimed it, although no town crier announced what was happening.

Living as the Arapesh believed they had always lived, with the only past an age of fable, a timeless time away, in a place where every rock and tree served to reinstate and reaffirm that changeless past, the old, the middle-aged, and the young received and conveyed the same set of messages: that this is what it is to be human, to be a boy or a girl, to be a firstborn or a lastborn child, to be born into the clan of the eldest brother or the clan of a younger ancestor; that this is what it is to belong to the half of the village for whom the hawk is the patron bird and to be someone who will grow up to speak lengthily at feasts, or, if one is born or adopted into the other side of the village, to grow up as a cockatoo and to speak briefly. Equally, the child learned that many would not live to grow up. He learned that life is a fragile thing, that may be withheld from the newborn of unwanted sex, may flicker out in the arms of a nursing mother who loses her milk when her child cannot flourish on it, may be lost because a kinsman has been angered and has stolen some of one's body substance and given it to enemy sorcerers. The child learned, too, that the hold of

men on the land around them was slight and tenuous; that
there were deserted villages without people to live in them beneath the trees; that there were names of yams for which the
seed or the charms to grow them had been lost, and only the
names remained. Loss of this kind was not treated as a change,
but rather as a recurrent and expected state in a world where
all knowledge was fleeting and all valued objects were made
by other people and must be imported from them. The dance
that was imported twenty years ago had now been passed on
to a more inland village, and only the anthropologist standing
outside the system, or occasionally a member of a neighboring
group, convinced of the inferiority of the mountain people
and looking for a way to illustrate it, might comment on the
parts of the dance they had kept and those they had lost.

The sense of timelessness and all-prevailing custom that I
found among the Arapesh, with its slight overtones of despair
and a fear that knowledge might be lost for good and that
human beings who seemed smaller each generation might indeed disappear, is the more striking because they did not live,
as the inhabitants of isolated islands do, cut off from all other
peoples. Their villages stretched across a mountain range from
the beach to the plains. They traded with and traveled among
and entertained peoples who spoke other languages and practiced other but similar customs. This sense of identity between
the known past and the expected future is the more striking
where small changes and exchanges occur all the time. It is the
more striking in an area where so much can be exchanged—
pots and bags, spears and bows and arrows, songs and dances,
seeds and charms. Women did run away from one tribe to
another. There were always one or two strange women living in
the village who had to learn to speak the language of the men
who claimed them as wives when they came and hid in the men-
strual huts. This, too, was part of life, and the children learned
that other women later would run away. Boys learned that
someday their wives might run away; girls learned that they
themselves might run away and have to learn different cus-

toms and a different language. This, too, was part of an un-changing world.

The Polynesians, scattered on remote islands, many hundreds of miles apart, settled where some small group had made a land-fall after weeks at sea, stripped of part of their possessions for-ever and with many dead, still were able to re-establish their traditional culture and add a special element to it—the deter-mination to preserve it, firmly anchored by genealogy and myth-ological authenticating parentage in the past. In contrast, the peoples of New Guinea and Melanesia, dispersing during many more thousands of years over small distances, within diversified habitats, have cherished and accentuated small differences, insisting that a few changes in vocabulary, a change of pace or a shift in consonants meant a new dialect, and have maintained their sense of changeless identity within a framework of con-tinuous interchange and small, noncumulative diversifications of custom.

We find postfigurative cultures surviving or reconstituted among peoples who have lived through tremendous and, in some fashion, remembered historical changes. The people of Bali have been subjected, over many hundreds of years, to pro-found foreign influences from China, from Hinduism, from Buddhism, from another and later form of Hinduism brought by the invading Javanese who were fleeing from Islamic con-querors. In the 1930s, in Bali, the ancient and the modern existed side by side in Balinese sculpture and dances, in the Chinese coins used for currency, in the western acrobatic dances imported from Malaya, and in the bicycles of the ice-cream vendors and the ice containers strapped to their handle bars. Outsiders and the occasional educated Balinese could discern the influence of the high cultures of the East and West, sort out the elements of ritual that belonged to different pe-riods of religious influence, and point out the differences be-tween the Brahmans who followed the Hindu Shivistic rites and those who were Buddhist in origin. The unsophisticated keeper of a low-caste temple in a Balinese village could do this too; he would shift the names he habitually called the village gods from such simple and proper appellations as Betara Desa, god of the village, to the name of a Hindu high god when a high-caste visitor was present. Each village had its individual style, its temples, its trances, and its dances; villages dominated by one high-caste group differed from others dominated by another caste. Yet two firmly held ideas pervaded Bali that the people reiterated in endless, tireless succession: "Every Balinese village is different"; and "All of Bali is the same." Although they had ways of recording the passing of the years and occasionally monuments were dated, the calendar they lived by was one of cycling days and weeks, with celebrations marking the recurrent coincidence of certain combinations of weeks. A new palm-leaf book, when a copy was finished—for new books were copies of other books made long ago—was dated by the day and week, but not by the year. Changes, which in Melanesia would differentiate a people from their neighbors, which in Polynesia would be denied and reduced, and which in a culture devoted to the idea of change and progress would be treated as genuine innovations—such changes were treated in Bali simply as changing fashions within a recurrent and essentially unchanging world into which infants were reborn within their own families to have a fortunate or an unfortunate life.

The Balinese have a long, rich, highly diversified history of diffusion, immigration, and trade, and yet Balinese culture as certainly as that of the primitive Arapesh, remained a postfigurative culture until World War II. The rituals of life and death and marriage repeated the same theme. The ritual drama depicting the struggle between the dragon, who represented life and ritual, and the witch, who represented death and fear, was enacted as mothers played age-old teasing games with the children they held in their arms. The witch carried the cloth in which a mother held her baby; the dragon, stripped of his teeth and fiery tongue, which dragons usually wear, sheltered his followers within his harmless jaws as he enacted the playful Balinese father's role. There was no break between the experience of the old and the experience of the young. No expectation of change or difference reached the child as it relaxed or tensed with fear and delight in the arms of its mother, who relived her earlier experience in the arms of her own mother, as she watched the witch with her magic cloth throw her attackers, supine, into a trance.

This quality of timelessness is found even among peoples whose ancestors belonged to great civilizations whose members were fully conscious of the possibilities of change. Some immigrants from Europe to America, especially those who shared a cult belief, settled in the New World and purposefully established communities which re-established the same sense of timelessness, and of inescapable identity from one generation to another. Hutterites, Amish, Dunkards, Sikhs, Dukhobors all display these qualities. Even today, in such communities, the children are reared so that the life of the parents and grandparents postfigures the course of their own lives. So reared, it is almost impossible to break away; a break means, inwardly as well as outwardly, such a change in the sense of identity and continuity that it is like a rebirth—rebirth into a new culture.

Under the pressure of contact with cultures which are not postfigurative, or are both postfigurative and missionizing, making absorption a part of their own cultural identity, individuals may leave their own culture and enter another. They bring with them the sense of what cultural identity is and the expectation that in the new culture they will strive for identity just as they did in the old. In many instances they merely assign parallel meanings, speaking the new language with the syntax of the old, treating dwellings as interchangeable but decorating or entering the house in the new society as they would have done in the old. This is one of the familiar types of adjustment made by adult immigrants from a postfigurative culture when they enter a strange society. Their internal integration does not change; it is so firm that a great number of mere substitutions of items can be made without loss of identity. Then there comes a time for many adult immigrants when there will be an accumulation of such interchanged items.

It is not yet known whether this kind of transformation is possible for persons coming from a culture without some concept of transformation. Japanese who were born in America but who had been sent home for a long period of education in Japan and then had returned again to the United States (those Japanese who were called *kibei* in the difficult days of World War II) had little conflict about loyalty when the moment of choice came. They had learned that one must be loyal, but also that membership in a society can be lost and that allegiance can be changed. The fact they had been loyal and acknowledged Japanese meant that they were able to become loyal Americans. Their postfigurative indoctrination already contained the possibility of complete transfer to another society.

It is by some such process that we may understand what must have been in primitive times the life of California Indian women who, because of proliferating incest rules, could not marry within communities in which their own language was spoken and who had to go, as strangers, to live out their whole lives within another language group. Here there developed, over uncounted centuries, a woman's language and a man's language—within the same group. The expectation of contrast between the language and associated culture of one's mother and father became a part of the culture into which one was born, postfigured in the songs a grandmother sang and in women's conversation when they were alone. The newcomer to a tribe had learned from her mother and grandmother that women spoke a different language from men, and the man she married had learned to hear the women's language and to speak the men's. These expectations became part of the supporting expectations of the whole set of intermarrying but linguistically diversified peoples.

Just as postfigurative cultures may contain within them expectations of leaving and entering another culture, so also they may contain types of learning that make any such accommodation impossible. Ishi, the lone California Indian who was found in 1911 waiting for death as the sole survivor of a tribe which had been hunted to their death by white men, possessed no previous learning that could give him a full place in the white man's world. The identity he maintained was that of a Yana Indian, demonstrating to eager young anthropology students at the University of California how arrowheads were made by the Yana. His early education and his searing, traumatic experience of ten years of hiding from predatory white men contained no provision for change of his own group membership.

Richard Gould has recently studied desert-dwelling Australian aborigines who had been brought long miles from their own "country," where every bit of their part of the desert was known and invested with deep meaning, to a settlement station where more acculturated aborigines lived. The desert people initiated the method that Australian aborigines had used for countless generations to relate to the other tribes near them; they tried to fit their marriage system together with that of the more acculturated people. But the more acculturated aborigines, those who were partly losing their identity, who no longer hunted and made no sacred ceremonies, but who like their forebears, in the end seemed to resist acculturation, were wary of reciprocation. They showed the scars of past failure to come to real terms with the white man's culture. Australian aborigines had had no objection to a man from another tribe cohabiting with their women, providing that he observed the taboos which defined the marriage classes. But white men had no marriage classes; they had, instead, a deep sense of their own racial superiority. That the aboriginal women were sexually available was a sign of the indelible inferiority of the aborigines. In contact with white men, the aborigines lost their intricate and well-tried way of interdigitating their particular culture system with that of others, and the resulting paralysis halted acculturation.

The way in which children learn languages from their elders defines how as adults, they themselves will be able to learn new languages. They may learn each new language as a comparable system which makes transformations possible, as New Guinea peoples surrounded by groups speaking other languages do, as

Jews and Armenians have done. Or they may learn their own language as a uniquely correct system, of which all other systems are merely imperfect translations, as Americans have learned English, when they have been taught by teachers who have rejected the mother tongue of their elders.

So through the ages, children have been brought up in culturally evolved ways into which most but not all the children born within the society can be fitted. Distinctions are made among children in terms of observed individual differences and these are treated as categories into which all children must somehow be fitted. The Balinese distinguish between children who are naturally naughty and those who are naturally sober and virtuous. Very early in a Balinese child's life the decision is made as to which type he is; the attribution, whether it fits well or poorly, lasts through old age. The Samoans—and the French—make distinctions based on age, on the point at which the child attains a capacity to understand what goes on in his society. But no recorded cultural system has ever had enough different expectations to match all the children who were born within it. Sometimes the child who departs too far from expectations dies. Sometimes it is only stunted and angry or forced into an identification with the opposite sex; such children in turn may grow up to distort the responses of those around them. Neuroses, if we see them in the case of individuals as failures of the expected system of upbringing, occur in all known societies.

In all systems of upbringing, some provision has to be made for handling the conflict between the child's springing sexuality and its tiny size, its subordinate position and lack of maturity. Sometimes the cultural forms almost match part of the child's precocity, as in fishing and hunting societies, where small boys of five or six can learn their parents' subsistence skills and can marry as soon as they reach puberty. Sometimes extraordinary courage is demanded of very small boys, as for example, among the Mundugumor of New Guinea, who sent children as hostages to a temporarily allied tribe. The children were instructed to learn as much as they could while they were hostages, so that sometime later they could guide a head-hunting raid into the same village. In more complex societies however, in which adult roles are far beyond the reach of six- and seven-year-olds or even sixteen-year-olds, other methods have to be adopted to reconcile the children to the postpone-ment of maturity. Parents have to defend themselves against a re-arousal of their own long suppressed early childhood sex-uality. This may become a focus of indulgence, as when little Balinese boys are permitted to wander about in groups, un-kempt and unwashed and undisciplined, or when Bathonga small boys are sent to be reared by their mothers' brothers instead of by their stern fathers, or when Zuñi parents them-selves avoid conflicts with their children by combining seem-ing indulgence with secret invitations to the scare dancers to come and beat the naughty children.

So in every postfigurative society the reappearance in every generation of the oedipal challenge to male authority, which seems to have had biological efficacy in earlier forms of man, but in all known cultures is inappropriate in children too young for reproduction and responsibility, has to be met if the so-ciety is to survive. Children must not be treated in ways that exploit their premature responsiveness, so everywhere there are rules against incest. At the same time, adults must be pro-tected from the memories, fears and hostilities and despera-tions that are reactivated in themselves by their children and that may otherwise result in rejection and destruction of the children.

Every social system may also be expected to produce some felicitous exceptions—children to whom event after event con-veys a sense of special blessing and good fortune or of special election for deeds greater than those expected of their fellows. These may be institutionalized, as among American Indians, in those cultures in which adolescents and adults sought visions and men with compelling visions became leaders. This allow-ance for the occurrence of genius—that special combination of gifts of temperament, native endowment, and environmental emphasis—means that, when the times are also ripe in men and in ideas, individuals may be able to create new cultural forms by a vision—or a dream. The match between ability and felicity of experience is a function of the culture itself. In a culture in which ideas of invention and change are both lacking, a very specially gifted individual may be needed to introduce even a very minor change, such as a small change in the existing art style, in the use of a new raw material, or in the enlargement of the size of a war party. Such minute changes may require as great gifts as did the inventions of a Galileo or a Newton, who worked within the context of a great tradition of scientific growth in knowledge.

We still know very little about how such felicitous breaks in the system of obtaining conformity and replication occur. We do not know how it is that some children keep their spontaneity within systems that dull and discipline spontaneity, how some children learn to keep on wondering after all the accepted answers have been given or how they remain extravagantly hopeful in the face of routine conditions of hunger and despair. During the last half century we have learned a great deal about trauma, about the exposure of infants or children to events that they are unable or unprepared to bear, but we still know very little about those who are unusually blessed. This is one of the sets of conditions about which young people are asking questions.

Intergenerational relationships within a postfigurative society are not necessarily smooth. In some societies each generation is expected to rebel—to flout the expressed wishes of the old men and to take over power from men older than themselves. Childhood may be experienced as agonizing, and small boys may live in fear of being seized by elderly uncles and aunts who perform terrifying ceremonies in their honor. But when the same small boys are grown, they expect their brothers and sisters to carry out on behalf of their children the same ceremonial behavior that had so terrified or mortified them. In fact, some of the most stable postfigurative cultures, such as those of the Australian aborigines or the Banaro of the Keram River in New Guinea, are characteristic of societies in which the whole population is involved in a ritual of torture and initiation or of differential wife-sharing and sexual initiation, many facets of which can best be described as torture, arousing shame and terror in the recipients.

Just as the prisoner who has slept on a hard bed for many years dreams of a soft bed but finds, when he comes out of prison, that he can sleep only on a hard one, and as ill-fed people, who move to a place where better food is found, may still cling to the less nutritive and originally unappealing diets of their childhood, so also human beings seem to hold on more tenaciously to a cultural identity that is learned through suffering than to one that has been acquired through pleasure and delight. Children who have grown up happily in comfortable homes can be more secure and adaptable under new circumstances than those whose early lessons have been painful and frightening. The sense of cultural identity that is drilled in with punishment and threats of total rejection is curiously persistent. A sense of national identity, which is defined by suffering and the capacity to suffer, by pride in the earlier heroic suffering of one's ancestors, can be maintained in exile under circumstances that might be expected to dissipate it. A few tremendously durable communities, such as those of the Jews and the Armenians, have displayed a persistent sense of national identity through hundreds of years of persecution and exile.

But the prototype postfigurative culture is the isolated primitive culture, the culture in which only the accommodating memories of its members are there to preserve the story of the past. Among preliterate peoples, there are no books to lie quietly on the shelf to give the lie to some revision of past history. The voiceless stones, even when they are carved and shaped by the hand of man, can easily be fitted into a revised version of how the world has always been. Genealogists, unembarrassed by documents, condense history, so that the mythological and the recent past flow together. "That Julius Caesar! He had every man in this village out working on the roads!" "In the beginning was the void." To destroy the memory of the past or preserve it in a form that merely reinforces the different present has been a continuous and highly functional adjustment by primitive peoples, even those who have been most historically minded, as they have come to believe that their small group originated in the place where they now live.

It is on their knowledge of societies of this kind that anthropologists have drawn in developing the concept of culture. The apparent stability and sense of changeless continuity characteristic of such cultures is built into the model of "a culture," that anthropologists have presented to others, not anthropologists themselves, who wish to use anthropological concepts in the interpretation of human behavior. But there has always been an apparent contradiction between the way anthropologists have described small, primitive, homogeneous, slowly changing societies, and the diversity existing among primitive tribes inhabiting such regions as New Guinea and California. It is obvious that over time great changes, although within approximately the same technological level, must have occurred. Peoples separated, languages diverged. Peoples speaking the same languages have been found hundreds of miles apart; groups with strongly contrasting physical types have been found speaking the same language or sharing the same culture.

What has not been emphasized enough, I believe, is that when there is no written language, no documentation of the past, the perception of the new is rapidly engulfed by the style of the old. The elders who edit the version of the culture that is passed on to the young mythologize or deny change. A people who have lived for only three or four generations in tepees on the great American plains, who have borrowed the tepee style from other tribes, may tell how their ancestors learned to make a tepee by imitating the shape of a curled leaf. In Samoa the elders listened politely to a description of the long voyages of Polynesian ancestors by Te Rangi Hiroa, a Polynesian visitor from New Zealand, whose people had preserved a sacrosanct list of the early voyages which was memorized by each generation. His hosts then replied firmly, "Very interesting, but the *Samoans* originated here in Fitiuta." The visitor, himself half-Polynesian and half-European, and a highly educated man, finally took refuge, in great irritation, in asking them whether or not they were now Christians and believed in the Garden of Eden!

In blurring change and assimilating innovation into a distant past, the reliability of memory in relation to the known plays an important part. We have found that a people who can describe every detail of an event that occurred in a period of relative stability will give much more contradictory and imperfect accounts of events that occurred more recently during a period of greater instability. Events that have to be fitted into an unfamiliar setting take on an air of unreality, and in time, if they are remembered at all, they are fitted again into familiar forms, and the details of change, like the process of change, are forgotten. Continuity is maintained by the suppression of memories that disturb the sense of continuity and identity.

Even in cultures in which the idea of change has been incorporated, the use of detail to flesh out the memory of events, whether they are distant or recent in time, serves to preserve a sense of continuity over very long periods. Although this is a technique that may be lost together with the attitudes toward identity and continuity to which it is related, it can also be regained. The persistent, unquestioning sense of identity and of the pervasive rightness of each known aspect of life, characteristic of postfigurative cultures, can occur—and can be reconstituted—at every level of cultural complexity.

Immigrants, coming to a new country like North America or Australia from another in which literacy is thousands of years old and every ancient town is graced by buildings that proclaim a historical sequence of change, may lose the very idea of change. Without the old records and the old landmarks, the marketplace, the tree or the mountain around which history clustered, the past is condensed. The style of living in the new country, in which much of the past is preserved, is itself relevant. The fact that people go on speaking the old language and follow some of the old occupations—planting grapes in similar soil, sowing wheat in comparable fields, building houses that retain the old proportions—and that the landscape and even the night, in which the Dipper wheels across the same northern sky, are familiar, all this can give the immigrant community a sense of unbroken continuity. And this may carry as long as people live together in a group where the grandparents are still regarded as authorities and their recipes for the care of crops or the preservation of food and the proper handling of adversity is adhered to. In the Scandinavian communities of northern Minnesota, people who had come so far to continue a way of life preserved a great deal of their culture.

The childhood culture may have been learned so completely unquestioningly and contact with members of other cultures may have been so slight, so hostile, or so contrasting that the individual's deep sense of who he is may be almost unalterable. There single individuals may live for many years among strangers, working, eating, and sometimes even marrying and rearing children, without questioning their identity or seeking to take on the new identity which, reciprocally, is not offered to them. Or whole groups may establish habits of limited migration, as in Greece or China. All the men may go away to sea when they are grown or they may go to work in the mines, the vineyards, or the factories of another country, leaving their women and children at home. Through the generations, new adaptations are made to the absence of fathers, but the culture, although altered, can still be transmitted coherently.

But the possibilities of change are much greater when the group is transplanted to another environment in circumstances in which all three generations leave their homeland and move together to a place where the new landscape can be compared to the old—where rivers run or the sea pounds with the same sounds—and much of the old way of life has been preserved, so that the grandparents' memories and the children's experience flow together. The fact that in the new country it is already cold in early September where once one could sit in the sun until October, that there are no sunflower seeds for little cakes, that the berries gathered in the early summer are black instead of red, and that the nuts gathered in autumn

have a different shape though they are called by the old name—
all these variations introduce a new element into the grandparents' comments. "In the old country" it was different.

This awareness of difference opens the way to a new choice
for the child. He can listen and absorb the sense of there and
here as being different places, making the fact of migration
and change part of his consciousness. In so doing, he may cher-
ish the contrast and look with affection on the few mementos
of a previous different existence; or he may find these ancestral
memories burdensome or unalluring and reject them altogether.
The government of the new country may insist that immigrants accept a new ideology, give up the living habits of the
past, vaccinate their babies, pay taxes, send their young men
into the armed service and their children to school to learn
the state language. Even without such insistence there are other
pressures against listening to the old. If the tales the old tell
are too nostalgic—if they speak of the many storied houses in
which they once lived, as the Yemenites did when they were
brought to Israel; or romanticize the old snug peasant houses
as the Irish, trapped in city tenements, did—then the stories
of the grandparents breed discontent. Past grandeur is poor fare
for an empty pot and does little to keep the wind from whistling
through the chinks.

So it is not surprising that many peoples, even when they
are living together, in their own community, in the land to
which they have migrated, let much of the past go and exclude
from their narrowed lives much of the richness of their premi-
gration past. People who once shared that past, although mea-
gerly, as peasants or proletarians, let the echoes of past literacy
and history die, and settle down to live an attenuated life where
they now are. This was the kind of life lived by English-speaking
mountain people in parts of the American southeast. Their culture unmistakably derived from the British Isles. But groups
of people were found, at the outbreak of World War I, who had
never left their valleys, knew nothing of the country in which
they were living—not even the name of the nearest large town.
Yet once they had been part of a tradition in which the strug-

gles of kings and barons had been significant and men had migrated to a new world for religious and political reasons.

Such attenuations of an older culture, which was appropriate to a different habitat, a different form of livelihood, or a different-sized population, occur all over the world. There are South American Indians who know how to spin, but who spin only a kind of string to ornament their bodies, and do not weave. There are peoples among whom kinship has proliferated into the only form of social organization, whose ancestors were members of organized empires. There are peoples like the Mayans and the Cretans whose way of life, even in the same habitat, has become fragmented and who have lost much that was once intrinsic to their ancestors' culture.

All such changes alter the quality of the culture. We may, I think, make useful distinctions as to the nature of change and the point at which a break comes—the point at which one must cease to speak of a postfigurative culture and treat what now exists as a culture of a different type. The only essential and defining characteristic of a postfigurative culture, or of those aspects of a culture that remain postfigurative in the midst of great changes in language and in allegiance, is that a group of people consisting of at least three generations take the culture for granted, so that the child as he grows accepts unquestioningly whatever is unquestioned by those around him. In such circumstances the amount of culturally patterned and internally consistent behavior that is learned is enormous and only a very small part of it is made conscious: the cakes at Christmas are named and commented upon, but the amount of salt in the potatoes goes unremarked. The painted magical circles on the barns to keep the milk from souring are named, but the proportions of the hay mow and the milk shed are not mentioned. The preferential treatment given men and certain animals, the nuances of relationships between men and women, habits of rising and going to bed, the way money is saved and spent, responses to pleasure and pain—these are all great bodies of transmitted behavior, which, when analyzed, can be shown to be consistent and omnipresent, but they remain below the surface of consciousness. It is this unlabeled, unverbalized, and nonconscious quality that gives to the postfigurative culture, and to the postfigurative aspects of all cultures, great stability.

The situation of those who learn a new culture in adulthood may also have a large amount of postfigurative-style learning. No one actually teaches the immigrant from another country how to walk. But as a woman buys the clothes of her new country and learns to put them on—slips at first uncomfortably into clothes worn by the women she sees on the street and then accommodates herself to a dress style in which she must put the dress on over her head instead of stepping into it —she begins to acquire the posture and stance of women in the new culture. Other women respond to this also unconsciously; they begin to treat the newcomer more as an insider, less as a stranger, take her into the bedroom and into their confidence. As men put on the strange new clothes, they learn when they can and when they cannot stand with their hands in their pockets without arousing comment or causing offense. The process is cumulative and, in many ways, as apparently effortless and unconscious as the process through which a child learns whatever, in his culture, is not made the subject of special discipline and comment. The people among whom a stranger takes up residence question their own habitual behavior as little as do the elders who have lived all their lives within a single culture.

These two conditions, lack of questioning and lack of consciousness, seem to be the key conditions for the maintenance of a postfigurative culture. The frequency with which the postfigurative style has been re-established after periods of self-conscious turmoil and revolt suggests that this is a form that remains, in part at least, as available to modern man as it once was to his forebears thousands of years ago. All the discrepancies that lie exposed in the paraphernalia of script and history, archives and coded law, can be reabsorbed into systems that, since they are unquestioned and below the surface of consciousness, are also unassailable by analysis.

The closer such unanalyzed cultural behaviors are to those of the observer, the harder they are to discern, even by the practiced and highly trained observer. In World War II there was relatively small resistance, except among observers who had been using different styles of observation (the "old China hands," as they were called) to cultural analyses of Japan, China, Burma, or Thailand. But the same intellectuals, who were willing to accept analyses of Asian peoples or African peoples, objected strenuously and emotionally when cultural analysis was applied to European cultures that contained many unanalyzed elements that were similar to their own. In these circumstances the defenses against self-analysis that permit a member of any one Euro-American culture to think of himself as a freely acting culturally unconstrained individual, were raised against the analysis of a related, for example, German, Russian, or English cultural character.

Appropriately, also, the sudden recognition of a specific form of postfiguratively established cultural behavior, when it occurs within one's own setting, among people of one's own educational level, is especially illuminating. The unanalyzed belief that other people, who look very different physically, or live at a very different social level from oneself, are somehow different also in deeply hereditary ways, is a very persistent one however strongly people may declare their allegiance to the scientific statement that beliefs associated with race and class are learned, not carried in the genes. Whenever the range of consistent difference is great, people will resort to the genetic explanation. Most people feel that others, who are very different from themselves, must indeed have inherited such differences. So cultural differences become most real when the individual can finally accept a cultural explanation of inexplicable elements in the behavior of a French or German colleague whose physique is the same.

It is just these deep, unanalyzed, unarticulated consistencies that are learned from unquestioning elders or unquestioning members of a culture into which they have newly moved, that must be made available to analysis if an understanding of culture is to become both a part of the intellectual apparatus of the human sciences and part of the climate of opinion in which the human sciences can flourish. As soon as men knew that they were speaking a language different from the language spoken by their neighbors, that was learned by children and could be learned by strangers, they became able to learn second and third languages, to make grammars, to alter their own languages consciously. Language, in this respect, is simply the aspect of culture that has been recognized longest as separable from man's heredity. The task of understanding the whole of another culture, the deepest organization of the emotions, the most imperceptible differences in posture and gesture, is not a different one from that of understanding another language. But the task of analyzing a whole requires different tools—the implementation of the gifted analytic eye and ear by camera, tape recorder, and instruments of analysis.

Today we have spread out before us examples, the various forms of postfigurative cultures, of peoples who represent successive phases of man's history from hunting and gathering to the present. We have the concepts and the instrumentation with which to study them. And although primitive peoples, inarticulate peasants, and the deprived people of rural backwaters and urban slums cannot tell us directly all that they see and hear, we can record their behavior for later analysis, and we can also put into their own hands a camera so that they can record and so help us see what we, by virtue of our upbringing, cannot see directly. Man's known past lies open before us, to inform us as, after a millennium of postfigurative and of cofigurative culture, during which men learned old things from their parents and new things from their peers, we have arrived at a new stage in the evolution of human cultures.

CHAPTER TWO

THE PRESENT

Cofigurative Cultures and Familiar Peers

A cofigurative culture is one in which the prevailing model for members of the society is the behavior of their contemporaries. Although there are records of postfigurative cultures in which the elders provide the model for the behavior of the young and in which there has been as yet no break in the acceptance of the ways of the ancestors, there are few societies in which cofiguration has become the only form of cultural transmission and none is known in which this model alone has been preserved through generations. In a society in which the only model was a cofigurative one, old and young alike would assume that it was "natural" for the behavior of each new generation to differ from that of the preceding generation.

In all cofigurative cultures the elders are still dominant in the sense that they set the style and define the limits within which cofiguration is expressed in the behavior of the young. There are societies in which approbation by the elders is decisive for the acceptance of new behavior; that is, the young look not to their peers, but to their elders, for the final approval of change. But at the same time, where there is a shared expectation that members of a generation will model their behavior on that of their contemporaries, especially their adolescent age mates, and that their behavior will differ from that of their parents and grandparents, each individual, as he successfully embodies a new style, becomes to some extent a model for others of his generation.

Cofiguration has its beginning in a break in the postfigurative system. Such a break may come about in many ways: through a catastrophe in which a whole population, but particularly the old who were essential to leadership, is decimated; as a result of the development of new forms of technology in which the old are not expert; following migration to a new land where the elders are, and always will be, regarded as immigrants and strangers; in the aftermath of a conquest in which subject populations are required to learn the language and ways of the conqueror; as a result of religious conversion, when adult converts try to bring up children to embody new ideals they themselves never experienced as children and adolescents; or as a purposeful step in a revolution that establishes itself through the introduction of new and different life styles for the young.

The conditions for change to a cofigurative type of culture became increasingly prevalent after the development of high civilization as access to greater resources, made it possible for the members of one society to annex, subjugate, incorporate, enslave, or convert members of other societies and to control or direct the behavior of the younger generation. Often, however, cofiguration, as a style, lasts only for a short period. In situations in which the cultural style of the dominant group is essentially postfigurative, second-generation members of a subjugated group (whose parents had no certain models except their peers) may be completely absorbed into a different, but still wholly postfigurative culture like the Israeli-born children in the kibbutz.

Nevertheless, the idea that it is possible to incorporate in a society a very large number of adults, differently reared and with different expectations, introduces a significant change into the culture of that society. Behavior is no longer so firmly associated with birthright membership in the society that it appears to be essentially inherited, rather than learned. Moreover, as the new groups which have been absorbed in the older population still maintain some parts of their own culture, it is possible to distinguish between the children of birthright members and the children of the newly absorbed. The idea that large numbers of individuals of different ages can be assimilated may produce a new flexibility and tolerance of difference.

But it may also stimulate the development of countermeasures, such as a firmer drawing of caste lines to ensure that the newcomers will be prevented from attaining the privileges of birthright members.

It is useful to compare different kinds of cultural absorption. Where absorption took the form of slavery, as a rule, large groups of adults were forcibly removed from their own homeland. They were denied the right to follow most of their own customs and their behavior was regulated by those who enslaved them. Primitive African societies practiced slavery on a large scale. Enslavement was used as a punitive measure within the society; but even slaves coming from other groups were culturally and physically similar to those who enslaved them. In many cases the slaves had rights that could not be denied them. And within a relatively short period the families and descendants of the enslaved were absorbed into the free society. The stigmata of slavery remained a blemish on the family line and various subterfuges might be resorted to as a way of escaping the past, but no significant difference of culture or appearance limited the participation of the descendants of slaves in the culture into which they were born.

Immigration to the United States and to Israel typifies the kind of absorption in which the young are required to behave in ways that are at sharp variance with the cultural behavior of their forebears. In Israel, immigrants from Eastern Europe placed the elderly—grandparents who accompanied their adult children—on the shelf. They treated them with the lessened respect accorded those who no longer have power and with a kind of negligence that emphasized the fact that the elderly are no longer the custodians of wisdom or models for the behavior of the young.

In a postfigurative culture the young may shudder away from the infirmities of the old or they may yearn for the wisdom and power the old represent; in both cases, they themselves will become what the old now are. But for the descendants of immigrants, whether the migration was voluntary or carried out under compulsion and whether the old people resolutely turned their backs on poverty and oppression or yearned for the life that once was theirs, the grandparents represent a past that has been left behind. Looking at their grandparents, the children see men and women whose footsteps they will never follow, but who are, by virtue of the tie through the parents, the people they would have become in another setting.

In slowly changing societies, the small recognizable changes in behavior by which one generation is differentiated from the next can be handled as changes in fashion, that is, as unimportant innovations by the young in matters of dress, manners, or recreation about which the old do not bother. In New Guinea, where peoples continually borrow or trade new styles from one another, all the women of a tribe, young and old alike, may adopt a new fashionable style of grass skirt, long in front and short behind (instead of short in front and long behind) or else the old women, who continue to wear the old outmoded skirts, may be firmly branded as old-fashioned. Minor variations within a prevailing cultural style do not essentially change the situation. In either case girls know that they will do whatever their grandmothers have done. When they are grandmothers they, too, will take up new fashions or, alternatively, they will leave it to the young to try out successive new fashions. The idea of continuity underlies the idea of fashion. The emphasis on fashion affirms that nothing important is changed.

In New Guinea cultures, no discrimination is made between changes that have a deep relationship to the core of the culture and superficial changes that may be made many times in a lifetime without touching the core. Throughout the area there is an essential homogeneity in the traits that are available for borrowing and abandonment, and many elements that are passed from tribe to tribe have followed the same course before. Analysis of New Guinea cultures demonstrates how continuous small changes at the surface can, in fact, produce great continuity and stability at deeper levels.

In contrast, the situation in which cofiguration occurs is one in which the experience of the young generation is radically different from that of their parents, grandparents, and other older members of their immediate community. Whether the young are the first native-born generation of a group of immigrants, the first birthright members of a new religious cult, or the first generation to be reared by a group of successful revolutionaries, their progenitors can provide them with no living models suitable for their age. They themselves must develop new styles based on their own experience and provide models for their own peers. The innovations made by the children of pioneers—those who first entered the new land or the new kind of society—have the character of adaptiveness which the elders, heedful of their own inexperience in the new country or their lack of past experience in the new religious or postrevolutionary world, can interpret as a continuation of their own purposive activity. The elders did, in fact, migrate; they cut down the trees in the forest or tamed the desert and built new settlements in which children, growing up, would have new opportunities for development. And these partially oriented adults, though they may take false cues from bird songs and seasons, can glory in the better habituation of their children.

Conflict between generations in such situations is not initiated by the adults. It does arise when the new methods of rearing the children are found to be insufficient or inappropriate for the formation of a style of adulthood to which the first generation, the pioneers, had hoped their children would follow.

Pioneers and immigrants who came to the United States, Canada, Australia, or Israel had no precedents in their own experience on which, without conscious thought, they could base the way they reared their children. How much leeway should parents give children? How far should they be allowed to wander from home? How could they control them, as they had been controlled by their fathers, by threats of disinheritance? Yet as the young grew up in these new situations, forming firm bonds among themselves, struggling with new conditions in the outer world and with obsolescent precedents in the minds of all their parents, their modeling on one another might still be well below the level of articulateness. In the United States, as one son after another, in one home after another, disagreed with his father and left home to go West or to some other part of the country, the circumstance that these battles were recurrent in most households came to have the appearance of the natural order of relations between fathers and sons.

It is possible that in societies in which there is strong opposition between generations, expressed in an insistence on separate living arrangements or in protracted symbolic conflict as control changes hands, the conflict originated in some major environmental shift. Once incorporated in the culture and taken for granted, such conflicts became part of the postfigurative culture. Great-grandfather left home; so did grandfather and, in his turn, father. Or, inversely, grandfather hated the school to which his father sent him; father also hated it, but in turn sent his son to school, fully expecting him to hate it. The occurrence of a generation break, in which the younger generation, lacking experienced elders, must take their cues from one another is a process that is very old in human history and will recur in any society as the aftermath of a break in the continuity of experience. Such a cofigurative episode may then be absorbed as the institution of age grading or the institutionalization of rebellion at a certain stage in maturation.

The situation is a very different one, however, when the parental group has to face a change in their children and grandchildren to a kind of behavior that already is exemplified by members of some other group—a conquering society, a dominant religious or political group, or the long-time inhabitants of the nation into which they have come as immigrants or of the city into which they have moved as migrants. In this situation they are constrained, by external force or by the strength of their own desires, to encourage their children to become part of the new order—to let their children leave them—by learning the new language, new habits, and new manners, which, from the parents' viewpoint, may have the appearance of a new set of values.

The new heritage is presented to the children by elders who are not their parents, grandparents, or members of their own transplanted or birthright settlements. Often the children have little access to the full home life characteristic of the culture to which they are asked to accommodate themselves, and their parents may have none. But as they go to school or to work or are conscripted into the army, they come in contact with peers with whom they can compare themselves. These peers present them with more practical models than those of the elders, the officers, teachers, and officials whose past is inaccessible to them and whose future it is difficult for them to see as their own.

In such situations the new entrants find that their peers, who belong to the system, are the best guides. This is the case in an institution, such as a prison or a mental hospital, in which there is a marked break between the inmates or patients and the powerful administrators and their delegates. In such institutions it is usually assumed that the personnel—doctors and nurses, warders and other custodians—are very different from the patients and prisoners. So newcomers model their behavior on that of older patients and prisoners.

In a caste society like that of traditional India, in which there was mobility within a caste but none between castes, members of different castes lived in close proximity within an essentially postfigurative culture. The impossibility of crossing caste lines—of acquiring the status, prerogatives, and standards of behavior of members of other castes—made it possible for the child firmly to incorporate both what he could not be and what he could be in his conception of his identity. In most societies a similar effect is attained in the upbringing of boys and girls. Members of each sex incorporate the behavior of the opposite sex as a negative ideal and reject it for themselves. In these circumstances, any crossing of sex lines—as when a man chooses an occupation that is regarded as feminine (and so effeminate for a man) or a woman attempts to take up a masculine occupation—produces a turmoil of generational conflict.

However, in class societies in which there is a high expectation of mobility, problems of generation conflict are endemic. The young person who is moving away from the position of his parents, whether they are peasants, or members of the middle class in an aristocratic society, or members of a subordinate racial or ethnic group, must openly and consciously forsake the postfiguration provided by his parents and grandparents and seek new models. This may be accomplished in various ways. In some societies, for example, in which it is customary for a small number of villagers or peasants to go to the city and learn city ways, those who do so treat urban modes of behavior as parallel to, rather than competitive with, rural modes and do not break the ties with their own upbringing. After years of city living, the petty official retires to his original home, there to live out his days eating the same food and following the same practices as his father before him did.

But in most class societies changes in occupation and status that entail modifications of behavior also involve changes in character structure as well. Normally the first break with the parental style comes about in connection with education, when parents elect a different type of education and a new occupational goal for their children. The outcome, however, is determined by the situation. When the number of such young people is large, they become models for one another and, rejecting the behavior models of adults in the new environment, treat teachers and administrators as opposition forces to be outwitted, not followed. But when the number of novices or students or recruits involved in change is small, the behavior of the majority becomes their model. Or an isolated adolescent may cling to one teacher who in some measure can provide support and guidance toward an adult path.

This kind of passionate attachment to an adult mentor can provide great depth, but it may also alienate the young individual from his own age group. He not only fails to approximate closely the behavior of his new peers, but also gives up the behavior appropriate to those of his own class or cultural group. He does not fit fully into his new setting and, returning to his place of origin, cannot reestablish ties there. In contrast, boys and girls who have entered enthusiastically into the new pursuits of school and college and who are at ease with their own age mates, when they return home for short periods may be able to transfer that sense of ease to those at home. An isolated, adult-fixated student, returning to his home, will seem alien to his fellows; but a group of schoolboys who have developed their own style may become models for their younger brothers—and sisters also—who will find it "natural" to follow in their footsteps.

The irruption into any age class of outsiders having a different past experience inevitably will produce changes in the army, school, or monastery system; often the entire age group will come to have goals distinctly different from those of their officers, teachers, or novice masters. The newcomers may import a style of behavior that is incongruent with the approved and expected behavior of birthright members. Or, introducing new slang and new points of view, they may develop variations on the birthright style and become models for their birthright companions. In any event, cofigurative behavior in which neither past nor future is clearly envisioned and all behavior is regulated by clique or group behavior is inevitably shallow and somewhat dissociated from the postfigurative experience of childhood. Where periods away from home, designed to break the ties between adolescents and their parents and local groups, have become a standardized preparation for specific occupations, this disassociation itself becomes institutionalized. The English boarding-school boy finds it impossible to communicate very much about his school experience, even though he knows his father's experience was identical. The very identity of the experience may make it a barrier between father and son.

Students of adolescence stress the conformity characteristic of this age. But the conformity they discuss occurs in one of two types of culture—the culture in which cofigurative behavior has been institutionalized for many generations, for example, in a society with institutionalized age grading; or, in contrast, the culture in which the majority of adolescents, finding no models in the behavior of parents whose experience is alien to theirs, must depend heavily on all the small external cues that can give them a sense of membership in a new group.

In its simplest form, a cofigurative society is one in which there are no grandparents present. Young adults, migrating from one part of a country to another, may leave their parents behind them, or they may leave them in the old country when they emigrate to a new one. Grandparents also are likely to be absent in a modern, mobile society like the United States, in which both old and young move frequently, or in industrialized, highly urban societies in which the affluent or the very poor segregate the elderly in special homes or areas.

The transition to a new way of life, in which new skills and modes of behavior must be acquired, appears to be much easier when there are no grandparents present who remember the past, shape the experience of the growing child and reinforce, inarticulately, all the unverbalized values of the old culture. The absence of grandparents usually also means the absence of a closed, narrow ethnic community. In contrast, when grandparents are part of a group immigrating into an alien society, the close ties within a village community may serve to keep the immigrant community intact.

When young adults strike out for themselves and form new ties appropriate to a new style of life, the ties among cousins also are weakened. It is ties through the ancestral group that keep alive contacts among the younger generation. In the United States, living aunts and uncles, by keeping up relationships with their nephews and nieces, also preserve the relationships among cousins. When they die, cousin relationships attenuate.

With the removal of the grandparents physically from the world in which the child is reared, the child's experience of his future is shortened by a generation and his links to the past are weakened. The essential mark of the postfigurative culture—the reversal in an individual's relationship to his child or his relationship to his own parents—disappears. The past, once represented by living people, becomes shadowy, easier to abandon and to falsify in retrospect.

The nuclear family, that is the family that consists only of parents and children, is in fact a highly flexible social group in situations in which a large portion of a population, or each generation in succession, must learn new ways of living. It is easier to adapt to the life style of a new country or to make new adaptations when immigrants or pioneers, separated from their parents and other senior relatives, are surrounded by others of their own age group. So, also, the receiving society can draw on individuals coming from many cultures as immigrants, when all the newcomers are learning the new language and the new technology and can reinforce one another's commitment to the new way of life.

In large organizations that must change, and change quickly, retirement is a social expression of the same need for flexibility. The removal of senior officers and elderly personnel, all those who in their persons, their memories, and their entrenched relationships to their juniors, reinforce obsolescent styles, is parallel to the removal of grandparents from the family circle.

Where grandparents are absent or lose their power to control, the young may ostentatiously ignore adult standards or assume a mien of indifference to them. The adolescent enacts his limited and labeled role with the next younger group as his audience, and full cofiguration is established in which those who provide the models are only a few years older than those who are learning.

This is happening today in New Guinea in the Manus villages in the Admiralties. In 1928, the young men who went away to work as unskilled indentured laborers on their return were reabsorbed into the community; they were models only in the sense that, like them, younger boys wanted to go away to work and expected to return. Nowadays, however, the homecoming schoolboys and girls, with their school clothes, their transistor radios, their guitars and school books, give a coherent picture of a different life. Although there are now village schools, it is the returning boarding-school adolescents who are the models for the younger boys and girls. Although the adults approve, they can do little to help the children establish the radically new forms of behavior.

In the Iatmul village of Tambunam in New Guinea, where I worked in 1938 and briefly in 1967, adolescents and young men have gone away to work for Europeans for more than fifty years. In the past they almost always went in small groups, as recruiters coming to the village "bought" eight or ten boys from complacent elders or as a group of friends ran away over their elders' protests. On plantations, in the mines, on ships, they were initiated by other work boys, who were also part of a temporary, age-graded group, all of them far away from their villages. Here the younger boys, who had been recruited for a three-year period, entered a completely cofigurative society, the canons of which were expressed in a new language, Pidgin English (now called Neo-Melanesian). Their two worlds—the work-boy world and the village home—remained distinct, and when they returned home they were reabsorbed, although with increasing difficulty, into the slowly changing life of their own villages. The disassociated nature of the work-boy experience was illustrated by their accounts of it. The three years during which they conformed in dress, manners, and behavior to the work-boy style were summed up in a few brief sentences. In contrast, every detail of their terrain and way of life, including their memories of the past when their fathers still took part in head-hunting raids, was revivified as they approached home.

As the years went by, little colonies of Iatmul men were formed in the larger towns; now a few men are even taking their wives and children with them. Young men not only go away to work or to sell their carvings, but also to visit. They are beginning to find in the distant towns a small society into which they can be initiated by elders and age mates who shared the postfigurative experiences of their childhood.

Tambunam is a postfigurative culture in which men, proud of their past, set high standards both for themselves and for the school children, who, they believe, will be taught by white teachers to live as white men do. Each generation of men has adapted to change, but none has lost the sense of continuity.

Mbaan, one of the oldest men in the village, was a work boy before World War I. Today he remains a completely traditional figure, a great expert in the old ways who also speaks fluent Neo-Melanesian and who says explicitly that when his generation has died the past, too, will have died.

Tomi, the political leader of the village thirty years ago, had a quite different experience. He had worked, not as a work boy on a plantation, but in the home of Mrs. Parkinson, the part-Samoan wife of Richard Parkinson, the author of *Dreisig Jahre in der Südsee*. Mrs. Parkinson had helped establish a style that was transitional between the past and the new German colonial style. His experience in her model household might have turned Tomi into an expatriated native who married and lived away from home. Instead, he returned to Tambunam, where he became politically powerful. He was adamantly opposed to the mission and the proposed mission school, but he set a precedent of good relations with government. He not only spoke Neo-Melanesian fluently, but also had gained from his isolated experience an ease of communication with white men and enjoyment in managing their affairs. In 1938 he acted as our principal executive officer in the village.

In 1967, Kami Asavi, who had been the smallest boy in our household in 1938, immediately assumed Tomi's role in organizing the household we were setting up. Immediately after World War II, Kami Asavi had carried considerable responsibility as a member of the native police force charged with rounding up Japanese prisoners. Like Tomi, in whose household he had grown up as a young kinsman, he learned to enjoy an executive position among white men, but felt that his deepest ties were to his own society. He was Tomi's chosen successor. After Tomi's death, when he took over the position of village leader, he lined up the children and marched them off to school. Just as he belonged to the past, in his own eyes, they belonged to the future. School, not a model created by the young for themselves, was the way to that future. Tambunam is moving slowly through change, but the elders, even now, are not consciously supporting a transition stage.

The course of change among the Manus people of the Admiralty Islands contrasts with that of the Iatmul. The Manus, a seagoing people, already vigorously attuned to taking what they wanted in material things from their neighbors, transformed their own culture. When I studied them in 1928, I expected them to acquire a deteriorated version of the widespread shallow culture of New Guinea work boys. Instead, in 1946, after their exposure to the Japanese and the Allied armed forces in World War II, they began to redesign their own culture and moved all three generations into their own version of Euro-American culture.

The new Manus culture was unusual in that it made it possible for the whole society, transformed by a set of rules designed by its own members, to skip thousands of years. But it was not what I have called a prefigurative culture, as the Manus thought they were modeling their culture on one already in existence. Each small change was conceived as a way of acquiring Euro-American, often specifically American, social forms. Moreover, the whole society moved at once; unlike societies in which the elder generation is disallowed, abandoned, or eliminated, the Manus were able to accomplish a kind of change that is unprecedented in history. Within twelve years after the establishment of the first school, they were contributing teachers, clerks, interpreters, and nurses to the Territory and were sending their first students to the new University of Papua and New Guinea. By including the grandparents within the design for change, they retained the strength of a postfigurative culture that was particularly well adapted to change.

Concentration on the nuclear family, from which the grandparents have been eliminated and in which ties to all kin are very much weakened, is typical in immigration situations in which large numbers of people move great distances or have to adapt themselves to new, greatly contrasting styles of life. In time this emphasis on the nuclear family becomes incorporated in the new culture; even when grandparents are present, their influence is minimized. It is no longer expected that grandparents will be models for their grandchildren or that parents will have firm control over adult children's marriages or careers. The expectation that children will go away from or beyond their parents—as their own parents have done—becomes part of the culture.

When those who move to the city or to a colony overseas are all members of one culture, the locus of power is not the elders, who are disregarded, but a younger age group, and the first generation of adapted children set a style that may perpetuate a thinner version of the older culture. In this kind of cofiguration, the loss of the grandparents is not compensated for. When the adults who made the transition reach grandparental age, they do not reconstitute, except in isolated cult groups or aristocracies, the lost three-generation organization. The new culture often lacks depth and variety and, to the extent that it does, as in many ethnic enclaves in the United States or Argentina, may be less flexible and less open to adaptive change than the old postfigurative culture was. Evidence of this is found in the well-known narrowing of the colonial imagination, in the preservation of archaic forms of speech, in the reinstatement of kin ties on a generational basis and in the rejection of the stranger.

In old and very complex societies, postfigurative cults or sects survive in spite of drastic social change. One example is the hobbyhorse cult in England, in which participants wear masks reminiscent of the most primitive cultures and carry out practices handed down from one generation to the next for hundreds of years. In England and elsewhere such survivals exist side by side with the customs of the mid-twentieth century.

Over and over again in history, ways have been found to stabilize a culture within a new environment. In time, of course, there will always be a grandparental generation present, but new ways may be found of disregarding the elderly. So, for example, the technology and ceremonialism of Eskimo culture did not require the knowledge or esoteric wisdom of the elders. The Eskimo style of distant travel and visiting from one family to another made essential the development of very rapid and efficient means of orienting a hunter to a new territory. Unlike Australian aborigines, whose style of learning depended on lifelong knowledge of one territory and the endowment of that territory with tremendous supernatural significance, the Eskimo developed a style of communicating information rapidly that permitted them to move freely and easily into new territory. The old men were not needed as a repository of knowledge. Eskimo society was based on a two-generation group. When the old became a burden and a threat to the survival of the young, they themselves elected to die. Comparably, in the United States or Great Britain, at an extreme remove technologically from the Eskimo, the coal miner who has passed his prime has no active role in the limited, controlled communities inhabited exclusively by miners.

In pre-World War I Poland, the landed peasant would turn over the land to his married son in return for assurances that he would care for the old couple for life. But these assurances sometimes proved to have no binding power, and the old couple might be turned out to wander as beggars on the roads.

The ease with which many second- and third-generation Americans relinquish all responsibility for the elderly is related to the loss of sanctions. The breakdown of sanctions once exercised by the old, who retained control of property until they died, may mean that the position of the old is never restored. Similarly, where the old, because of better medical care, continue to live far beyond their expected lifetime, they may be shorn of responsibilities the next generation is more than ready to take over. Each such adaptive shift carries with it possibilities of change and a reduction of the depth characteristic of postfigurative cultures.

Under conditions of rapid change in a new country or under new conditions, men and women may relate to change in sharply contrasting ways. New ways of making a living may drastically affect the position of men who shift, for example, from full participation in a peasant community or from the narrow, controlled life of a rural sharecropper to the anonymous life of the urban unskilled laborer. But conditions may change very little for women, as they continue to cook and rear their children much as their mothers did. In these circumstances the parts of the culture that are transmitted by women in the course of forming the child's character in its early years may be conserved, while other parts of the culture, related to the drastically changed conditions of men's work, are radically altered and, in turn, lead to alterations in the character formation of children.

Cultures may be distinguished not only in terms of the relative importance of the roles played by grandparents and other kin, but also in terms of the continuity—or lack of continuity —in form of what is passed on from grandparent to parent to grandchild. For example, where there has been a shift in living style from one in which men married in and women remained close to their mothers to one in which daughters left their homes to live in their husbands' communities, evidence of this shift is found in discontinuities in handicraft styles. In contrast, the exceedingly conservative nature of styles of singing, evidence for which was found by Alan Lomax in his comparative studies of world song styles, can be attributed in part to the lullabies generations of mothers have sung to their children, unchanged in spite of massive changes in a people's way of life.

Conservatism in child rearing is characteristic of those cultures in which young children care for infants and the younger child is very close to the immediate past of the child nurse. The child nurse demands very little and demonstrates very little; she tends to carry her charge or drag him along with her instead of teaching him to fend for himself. In a highly complex culture, the peasant nurse, keeping the child close to his roots and minimizing stimulation, also is characteristically conservative in her influence.

When schools are first introduced into a society that has depended upon older children as child nurses, the culture may be disrupted in several ways. The older children are cut off from the daylong learning of traditional skills and are segregated under teachers the content and style of whose teaching may be entirely new. At the same time mothers have to take over the care of infants. This happens also, of course, when peasant women no longer are available to care for the children of the well-to-do. In both cases a new element enters the situation. Mothers and fathers, both of whom have other heavy responsibilities, are much more demanding of children, less patient and willing to keep them dependent and infantilized; in addition, the model they present to children is far more skilled and complex.

The existence of a caste component in the upbringing of children brings about a very complex interrelationship between the two groups. In the American southeast, where upper-class white children were reared by black nurses, white children acquired a sense of closeness to black people and the nurse learned to treat her charge differently from her own child. The kind of intimacy that existed within these two interacting groups was absent among others who, if they were white, employed no servants and, if they were black, did not work as domestic servants. Today, one of the conditions that has increased the distance and the expression of mutual hostility between blacks and whites is a new kind of segregation that has come about as fewer families employ servants and fewer black people have close contact with the white community as nurses or caretakers or as the recipients of care formerly tendered them by white nurses and doctors or other professional persons.

In the United States the conservative and stabilizing effects of old cross-caste and cross-class relationships are disappearing rapidly. Since World War II, changes in education, the refusal to perform menial work, and the opening of opportunities for entrance into other occupations, including professional occupations, and new residence patterns all have contributed to the general breakdown of older relationships between those who conform to the standards of the core culture and those who, for reasons of color, education, social isolation, or individual choice, refuse to conform.

Each culture selects for emphasis in child rearing only certain periods in the maturation of the growing child; which they are may differ in the several parts of one complex society. What is emphasized reflects the nature of the relationships between generations, as well as ages and classes within generations, and varies with the prevailing generation pattern. In a culture in which heavy stress is placed on early training in relation to food, the roles of the mother and grandmother are proportionately important. Where the boy's training in the control of his body and the development of manual skills begin early and are associated with the acquisition of masculine skills, the father and grandfather become important as soon as the boy learns to walk and talk. And to the extent that male and female personality is dichotomized, the treatment accorded boys and girls at the oedipal phase will be differentiated.

When a new cultural style is established among immigrants, when primitive or peasant peoples are brought within the direct control of national states, or when new levels of literacy and technological participation are forced on a people, the stage of development on which pressure appropriate to the new style of learning falls may be different from what it was in the past. A new pressure point may come when a young man leaves home to enter the national army, when the adolescent leaves a village school to enter a regional school, or when a child of six enters a village school designed on an alien model. Or the initial impact of change may come through methods of infant care promoted among young adults by emissaries of public health as they reach out into villages where few other changes are occurring.

Wherever cofiguration occurs—as young men are drilled to imitate fellow citizens, as boys in school are trained in new ways, or as school children are marched into village schools and educated to conform to a model developed far away in a different kind of society—the age and state of the initiates and the place and state of this group in the older postfigurative culture will be important. If the group already has incorporated the expectation of change through the upbringing of children, it may survive tremendous shifts, virtually unchanged. Or, as in the case of European Jews in the United States, the group may even accomplish a complete reversal. In the European style, fathers of daughters looked for promising sons-in-law; in the American style, promising young men look for the daughters of wealthy fathers. The greater the expectation of change, the less disruptive introduced cofigurations are likely to be.

As they adapted themselves to the American culture of their day, members of each non-English speaking group had to give up their own language and specific culture. The education of the children was the principal mechanism through which this was accomplished. The parents had no control over the new learning; indeed, in most cases, they had had no control over formal education in the countries from which they came. They had to entrust their children to the schools and accept their children's interpretation of what was correct American behavior. The children had for guidance only the precepts of their teachers and the examples of their age mates. In time, the experience of the children of immigrants became the experience of all American children, who now were the representatives of a new culture living in a new age. As such, they stood in a position of considerable authority and model setting vis-à-vis the parent generation.

The mere condition of rapid change can produce similar results. In nations such as India, Pakistan, or the new countries of Africa, children are also the authorities on the new ways and parents lose their power to judge and control. But where change occurs within a country, the combined weight of the old culture, the redintegrative power of old landmarks, and the presence of grandparents modulates the new authority claimed by the children. In countries of multi-ethnic immigration, however, the cofigurational effect is doubled and parents, displaced in time and space, find it doubly difficult to retain any control or even the belief that control is possible or desirable.

Where cofiguration among age mates has become institutionalized throughout the culture, one finds the phenomenon of youth culture or "teen-age" culture; age stratification, encouraged by the school system, becomes increasingly important. In the United States, the culture-wide effects of cofiguration began to be felt by the beginning of the twentieth century. The nuclear family was established, a close relationship to the grandparents no longer was expected of grandchildren, and parents, as they lost their position of dominance, handed over to children the task of setting their own standards. By 1920, style setting was beginning to pass to the mass media, in the name of each successive adolescent group, and parental discipline was passing to an increasingly unsympathetic and embattled community. One effect of this change, by the 1960s, was the transformation of some portion of the new generation of middle-class young people into a semblance of the ethnic gangs that, in an earlier period, had battled each other and the police in our big cities. Culturally, cofiguration had become the dominant, prevailing mode. Few of the elderly pretended to have any relationship to the contemporary culture. Parents, however grudgingly, expected to accede to the urgent demands their children were taught to make, not by the school or by other, more acculturated children, but by the mass media.

Societies that make deliberate use of the possibilities of cofiguration, by inducting adolescents or adults into groups in which they were not reared or trained, are often highly flexible in making new adaptations. To the extent that formal induction, such as occurs in various types of novitiate, in initiations, in the preliminary stage of training for service in the armed services or in training for the professions, is treated as a form of condensed childhood learning or, alternatively, as a total postfigurative experience, it is a highly successful mechanism for teaching and learning.

The individual who has grown up in a nuclear family, in which there is only a two-generation enforcement of early expectations, knows that his father and mother differ from his four grandparents and that his children will grow up to be different from himself. In contemporary societies there is the added expectation that childhood training will be at best only a partial preparation for induction into various groups other than the family. Taken together, living in a changing nuclear family and experiencing the effects of induction into new groups give the individual the sense of living in an ever-changing world. The more intense the experience of generational change in the family and of social change through involvement in new groups, the more brittle the social system becomes and the less secure the individual is likely to be. The idea of progress, which provides a rationale for the unstable situation, makes it bearable. It was the expectation of immigrant Americans that their children would be better educated and more successful than they were that supported them as they struggled with the difficulties of transition.

I have discussed the cofigurative elements of the pioneer generation type, in which adults must learn together to deal with a new situation, and the cofigurative elements of the second-generation type, in which the children of newcomers, the first natives in the new environment, must develop appropriate styles of behavior for which there are no parental models. I have indicated how pioneering situations can be regularized, so that age grading, youth rebellion, intergenerational conflict and the expectation that the children will regularly depart from the parental model are built into the culture. I have suggested how postfigurative cultures can be re-established, in the form of an isolated cult group that attempts to freeze the new model in perpetuity or, at a higher level of integration, through the formation of a major religion or a nation-state. Local versions of the new culture or the new religion may have strong cofigurative elements and carry on the expectation of generational change; but at the same time there is an overriding cultural assumption or religious conviction that what is, will endure without change.

I have defined a postfigurative culture as one in which much of the unchanging culture remains unanalyzed and which must be exemplified by three generations in continuing contact. In a society like our own, in which there is great social mobility, there are inevitably generation breaks in education and styles of living. Nevertheless, young people, as they move up and out, encounter certain values that are shared by most adults of the two older generations. Characteristically, these unchallenged beliefs, held by all adults, are unanalyzed, just as they are in postfigurative cultures. In an isolated society, it is relatively easy to re-establish a rigid adult consensus. But in the present-day interconnected world, it takes an iron or a bamboo curtain to assure a semblance of unanimity. Much more characteristic of contemporary societies is the disappearance of earlier forms of postfiguration. At the same time, recurrent attempts are made to re-establish unanalyzed consensus and unequivocal loyalty; or the followers of nativistic, revolutionary, or Utopian cults try to form closed communities as a way of establishing for all time some desired way of life.

Also characteristic of the modern world are the acceptance of generation breaks and the expectation that each new generation will experience a technologically different world. But this expectation does not extend to a recognition that the change between generations may be of a new order. For generations two cultural groups, Jews and Armenians, have reared their children to expect to move and to learn new languages without losing their sense of cultural identity. In much the same way, children in our own and many other cultures are being reared to an expectation of *change within changelessness*. The mere admission that the values of the young generation, or of some group within it, may be different in *kind* from those of their elders is treated as a threat to whatever moral, patriotic, and religious values their parents uphold with postfigurative, unquestioning zeal or with recent, postfiguratively established, defensive loyalty.

It is assumed by the adult generation that there still is general agreement about the good, the true, and the beautiful and that human nature, complete with built-in ways of perceiving, thinking, feeling, and acting, is essentially constant. Such beliefs are, of course, wholly incompatible with a full appreciation of the findings of anthropology, which has documented the fact that innovations in technology and in the form of institutions inevitably bring about alterations in cultural character. It is astonishing to see how readily a belief in change can be integrated with a belief in changelessness, even in cultures whose members have access to voluminous historical records and who agree that history consists not merely of currently desirable constructs but of verifiable facts.

Contemporary statements about man's plight or, alternatively, man's new opportunities do not envision the emergence of new mechanisms of culture change and culture transmission that differ fundamentally from the postfigurative and cofigurative mechanisms we are familiar with. Yet I believe a new cultural form is emerging; I have called it prefiguration. As I see it, children today face a future that is so deeply unknown that it cannot be handled, as we are currently attempting to do, as a generation change with cofiguration, within a stable, elder-controlled and parentally modeled culture in which many postfigurative elements are incorporated.

I believe that we can, and would do better to, apply to our present situation the pioneer model—the model of first-generation pioneer immigrants into an unexplored and uninhabited land. But for the figure of migration in space (geographical migration), I think we must substitute a new figure, migration in time.

Within two decades, 1940–60, events occurred that have irrevocably altered men's relationships to other men and to the natural world. The invention of the computer, the successful splitting of the atom and the invention of fission and fusion bombs, the discovery of the biochemistry of the living cell, the exploration of the planet's surface, the extreme acceleration of population growth and the recognition of the certainty of catastrophe if it continues, the breakdown in the organization of cities, the destruction of the natural environment, the linking up of all parts of the world by means of jet flights and television, the preparations for the building of satellites and the first steps into space, the newly realized possibilities of unlimited energy and synthetic raw materials and, in the more advanced countries, the transformation of man's age-old problems of production into problems of distribution and consumption—all these have brought about a drastic, irreversible division between the generations.

Even very recently, the elders could say: "You know, I have been young and *you* never have been old." But today's young people can reply: "You never have been young in the world I am young in, and you never can be." This is the common experience of pioneers and their children. In this sense, all of us who were born and reared before the 1940s are immigrants. Like first-generation pioneers, we were reared to have skills and values that are only partly appropriate in this new time, but we are the elders who still command the techniques of government and power. And like immigrant pioneers from colonizing countries, we cling to the belief that the children will, after all, turn out to be much like ourselves. But balancing this hope there is the fear that the young are being transformed into strangers before our eyes, that teen-agers gathered at a street corner are to be feared like the advance guard of an invading army.

We reassure ourselves by saying: "Boys will be boys." We rationalize, telling one another that "these are very unstable times," or that "the nuclear family is very unstable," or that "children are exposed to a lot of dangerous things on television." We say the same things about our children and about new countries that, as soon as they are established, demand an airline and an embassy in every world capital: "They are young and immature. They will learn. They will grow up."

In the past, in spite of generations of cofiguration and the wide acceptance of the possibilities of rapid change, there were extreme discrepancies in what was known by people of different classes, regions, and specialized groups in any country as well as in the experiences of peoples living in different parts of the world. Change was still relatively slow and un-even. Young people living in some countries and belonging to certain class groups within a country knew more than adults in other countries and belonging to other classes. But there were also always adults who knew more, in terms of experi-ence, than any young people.

Today, suddenly, because all the peoples of the world are part of one electronically based, intercommunicating network, young people everywhere share a kind of experience that none of the elders ever have had or will have. Conversely, the older generation will never see repeated in the lives of young people their own unprecedented experience of sequentially emerging change. This break between generations is wholly new: it is planetary and universal.

Today's children have grown up in a world their elders never knew, but few adults knew that this would be so. Those who did know it were the forerunners of the prefigurative cul-tures of the future in which the prefigured is the unknown.

CHAPTER THREE

THE FUTURE

Prefigurative Cultures and Unknown Children

Our present crisis has been variously attributed to the over-whelming rapidity of change, the collapse of the family, the decay of capitalism, the triumph of a soulless technology, and, in wholesale repudiation, to the final breakdown of the Establishment. Behind these attributions there is a more basic conflict between those for whom the present represents no more than an intensification of our existing cofigurative culture, in which peers are more than ever replacing parents as the significant models of behavior, and those who contend that we are in fact entering a totally new phase of cultural evolution.

Most commentators, in spite of their differences in view-point, still see the future essentially as an extension of the past. Teller can still speak of the outcome of a nuclear war as a state of destruction relatively no more drastic than the ravages wrought by Genghis Khan. Writing about the present crisis, moralists refer to the decay of religious systems in the past and historians point out that time and again civilization has survived the crumbling of empires.

Similarly, most commentators treat as no more than an extreme form of adolescent rebellion the repudiation of present and past by the dissident youth of every persuasion in every kind of society in the world. So Max Lerner can say "Every adolescent must pass through two crucial periods: one when he identifies with a model—a father, an older brother, a teacher—the second when he disassociates himself from his model, rebels against him, reasserts his own selfhood." There is little substantial difference between Lerner's view and that of David Riesman in his delineation of the autonomous man, who emerges from the present without too sharp a break with the past.

Perhaps the most extraordinary response to youthful rebellion has been that of Mao, who has attempted to turn the restive young against their parents as a way of preserving the momentum of the revolution made by the grandparent generation. Little as we understand the details of what has been going on in China, what we do know suggests a tremendous effort to transform the desire to destroy, which characterizes the attitudes of young activists all around the world, into an effective instrument for the preservation of the recently established Chinese Communist regime. If the Maoists succeed in this attempt, they will have made the most dramatic use of the techniques of temporary cofiguration to bring about a return to a postfigurative culture of which we have any record. There are indications that the modern Chinese may treat such new Western technologies as electronics as parallel to processes of assimilation that have occurred many times in the long history of Chinese civilization—no more significant than a new form of metallurgy.

Theorists who emphasize the parallels between past and present in their interpretations of the generation gap ignore the irreversibility of the changes that have taken place since the beginning of the industrial revolution. This is especially striking in their handling of modern technological development, which they treat as comparable in its effects to the changes that occurred as one civilization in the past took over from another such techniques as agriculture, script, navigation, or the organization of labor and law.

It is, of course, possible to discuss both postfigurative and cofigurative cultures in terms of slow or rapid change without specifying the nature of the process. For example, when the children of agricultural and handicraft workers entered the first factories, this marked the beginning of an irreversible change. But the fact that accommodation to this new way of living was slow, since it was spread out over several generations, meant that the changes were not necessarily perceived to be more drastic than those experienced by the peoples who were incorporated by conquest into the Roman Empire. So also, when attention is focused on generation relationships and on the type of modeling through which a culture is transmitted, it is possible to treat as fully comparable a past situation, as when a formerly land-bound people learned the techniques of fishing, and a present situation, as when the children of emigrant Haitians learn computer programming.

It is only when one specifies the nature of the process that the contrast between past and present change becomes clear. One urgent problem, I believe, is the delineation of the nature of change in the modern world, including its speed and dimensions, so that we can better understand the distinctions that must be made between change in the past and that which is now ongoing.

The primary evidence that our present situation is unique, without any parallel in the past, is that the generation gap is world wide. The particular events taking place in any country—China, England, Pakistan, Japan, the United States, New Guinea, or elsewhere—are not enough to explain the unrest that is stirring modern youth everywhere. Recent technological change or the handicaps imposed by its absence, revolution or the suppression of revolutionary activities, the crumbling of faith in ancient creeds or the attraction of new creeds—all these serve only as partial explanations of the particular forms taken by youth revolt in different countries. Undoubtedly, an upsurge of nationalism is more likely in a country like Japan, which is recovering from a recent defeat, or in countries that have newly broken away from their colonial past than it is, for example, in the United States. It is easier for the government of a country as isolated as China to order vast changes by edict than it is for the government of the Soviet Union, acting on a European stage, to subdue Czechoslovakian resistance. The breakdown of the family is more apparent in the West than in the East. The speed of change is more conspicuous and more consciously perceived in the least and in the most industrialized countries than it is in countries occupying an intermediate position. But all this is, in a sense, incidental when the focus of attention is on youthful dissidence, which is world wide in its dimensions.

Concentration on particularities can only hinder the search for an explanatory principle. Instead, it is necessary to strip the occurrences in each country of their superficial, national, and immediately temporal aspects. The desire for a liberal form of communism in Czechoslovakia, the search for "racial" equality in the United States, the desire to liberate Japan from American military influence, the support given to excessive conservatism in Northern Ireland and Rhodesia or to the excesses of communism in Cuba—all these are particularistic forms. Youthful activism is common to them all.

It was with the hope of turning anthropological analysis to this use that I tried to describe the essential characteristics of the postfigurative model and some of the forms taken by the cofigurative model under certain conditions of rapid change. It is my belief that the delineation of these models, as we have come to understand them through the study of older cultures, can help to clarify what is happening in the contemporary world.

The key question is this: What are the new conditions that have brought about the revolt of youth right around the world?

The first of these is the emergence of a world community. For the first time human beings throughout the world, in their information about one another and responses to one another, have become a community that is united by shared knowledge and danger. We cannot say for certain now that at any period in the past there was a single community made up of many small societies whose members were aware of one another in such a way that consciousness of what differentiated one small society from another heightened the self-consciousness of each constituent group. But as far as we know, no such single, interacting community has existed within archaeological time. The largest clusters of interacting human groups were fragments of a still larger unknown whole. The greatest empires pushed their borders outward into regions where there were peoples whose languages, customs and very appearance were unknown. In the very partially charted world of the past the idea that all men were, in the same sense, human beings was either unreal or a mystical belief. Men could think about the fatherhood of God and the brotherhood of man and biologists could argue the issue of monogenesis versus polygenesis; but what all men had in common was a matter of continuing speculation and dispute.

The events of the last twenty-five years changed this drastically. Exploration has been complete enough to convince us that there are no humanoid types on the planet except our own species. World-wide rapid air travel and globe-encircling television satellites have turned us into one community in which events taking place on one side of the earth become immediately and simultaneously available to peoples everywhere else. No artist or political censor has time to intervene and edit as a leader is shot or a flag planted on the moon. The world is a community though it lacks as yet the forms of organization and the sanctions by which a political community can be governed.

The nineteenth-century industrial revolution replaced the cruder forms of energy. The twentieth-century scientific revolution has made it possible to multiply agricultural production manyfold but also drastically and dangerously to modify the ecology of the entire planet and destroy all living things. Science has made possible, through the use of computers, a new concentration of intellectual efforts that allows men to begin the exploration of the solar system, and opens the way to simulations by means of which men, especially men working in organized groups, can transcend earlier intellectual accomplishments.

The revolution in the development of food resources is on a world-wide scale. Up to the present, in many parts of the world, the medical revolution has so increased the population that the major effect of increased, efficient food production has been to stave off famine. But if we are able to bring the human population into a new balance, all of humanity can be, for the first time, well nourished. The medical revolution by reducing

the pressure for population increase has begun, in turn, to re-
lease women from the age-old necessity of devoting themselves
almost completely to reproductivity and, thus, will profoundly
alter women's future and the future rearing of children.

Most importantly, these changes have taken place almost
simultaneously—within the lifetime of one generation—and
the impact of knowledge of the change is world wide. Only
yesterday, a New Guinea native's only contact with modern
civilization may have been a trade knife that was passed from
hand to hand into his village or an airplane seen in the sky;
today, as soon as he enters the smallest frontier settlement, he
meets the transistor radio. Until yesterday, the village dwellers
everywhere were cut off from the urban life of their own country; today radio and television bring them sounds and sights of
cities all over the world.

Men who are the carriers of vastly different cultural tradi-
tions are entering the present at the same point in time. It is
as if, all around the world, men were converging on identical
immigration posts, each with its identifying sign: "You are now
about to enter the post-World War II world at Gate 1 (or Gate
23 or Gate 2003, etc.)." Whoever they are and wherever their
particular point of entry may be, all men are equally immigrants into the new era—some come as refugees and some as
castaways.

They are like the immigrants who came as pioneers to a new
land, lacking all knowledge of what demands the new conditions of life would make upon them. Those who came later
could take their peer groups as models. But among the first
comers, the young adults had as models only their own tenta-
tive adaptations and innovations. Their past, the culture that
had shaped their understanding—their thoughts, their feelings,
and their conceptions of the world—was no sure guide to the
present. And the elders among them, bound to the past, could
provide no models for the future.

Today, everyone born and bred before World War II is such
an immigrant in time—as his forebears were in space—struggling to grapple with the unfamiliar conditions of life in a new

era. Like all immigrants and pioneers, these immigrants in time are the bearers of older cultures. The difference today is that they represent all the cultures of the world. And all of them, whether they are sophisticated French intellectuals or members of a remote New Guinea tribe, land-bound peasants in Haiti or nuclear physicists, have certain characteristics in common.

Whoever they are, these immigrants grew up under skies across which no satellite had ever flashed. Their perception of the past was an edited version of what had happened. Whether they were wholly dependent on oral memory, art, and drama or also had access to print and still photography and film, what they could know had been altered by the very act of preservation. Their perception of the immediate present was limited to what they could take in through their own eyes and ears and to the edited versions of other men's sensory experience and memories. Their conception of the future was essentially one in which change was incorporated into a deeper changelessness. The New Guinea native, entering the complex modern world, followed cultural models provided by Europeans and expected in some way to share their future. The industrialist or military planner, envisaging what a computer, not yet constructed, might make possible, treated it as another addition to the repertoire of inventions that have enhanced man's skills. It expanded what men could do, but did not change the future.

It is significant that mid-twentieth-century science fiction, written by young writers with little experience of human life, rang untrue to the sophisticated and experienced ear and was less interesting to most well-educated men than such myths as those of Icarus and Daedalus, which include men and gods as well as the mechanisms of flight. Most scientists shared the lack of prescience of other members of their generation and failed to share the dreams of modern science fiction writers.

When the first atom bomb was exploded at the end of World War II, only a few individuals realized that all humanity was entering a new age. And to this day the majority of those over twenty-five have failed to grasp emotionally, however well they may grasp intellectually, the difference between any war in which, no matter how terrible the casualties, mankind will survive, and one in which there will be no survivors. They continue to think that a war, fought with more lethal weapons, would just be a worse war; they still do not grasp the implications of scientific weapons of extinction. Even scientists, when they form committees, are apt to have as their goal not the total abolition of war, but the prevention of the particular kinds of warfare for which they themselves feel an uncomfortable special responsibility—such as the use of pesticides in Vietnam.

In this sense, then, of having moved into a present for which none of us was prepared by our understanding of the past, our interpretations of ongoing experience or our expectations about the future, all of us who grew up before World War II are pioneers, immigrants in time who have left behind our familiar worlds to live in a new age under conditions that are different from any we have known. Our thinking still binds us to the past—to the world as it existed in our childhood and youth. Born and bred before the electronic revolution, most of us do not realize what it means.

We still hold the seats of power and command the resources and the skills necessary to keep order and organize the kinds of societies we know about. We control the educational systems, the apprenticeship systems, the career ladders up which the young must climb, step by step. The elders in the advanced countries control the resources needed by the young and less advanced countries for their development. Nevertheless, we have passed the point of no return. We are committed to life in an unfamiliar setting; we are making do with what we know. We are building makeshift dwellings in old patterns with new and better understood materials.

The young generation, however, the articulate young rebels all around the world who are lashing out against the controls to which they are subjected, are like the first generation born into a new country. They are at home in this time. Satellites are familiar in their skies. They have never known a time when war did not threaten annihilation. Those who use computers do not anthropomorphize them; they know that they are programmed by human beings. When they are given the facts, they can understand immediately that continued pollution of the air and water and soil will soon make the planet uninhabitable and that it will be impossible to feed an indefinitely expanding world population. They can see that control of conception is feasible and necessary. As members of one species in an underdeveloped world community, they recognize that invidious distinctions based on race and caste are anachronisms. They insist on the vital necessity of some form of world order.

They live in a world in which events are presented to them in all their complex immediacy; they are no longer bound by the simplified linear sequences dictated by the printed word. In their eyes the killing of an enemy is not qualitatively different from the murder of a neighbor. They cannot reconcile our efforts to save our own children by every known means with our readiness to destroy the children of others with napalm. Old distinctions between peacetime and wartime, friend and foe, "my" group and "theirs"—the outsiders, the aliens—have lost their meaning. They know that the people of one nation alone cannot save their own children; each holds the responsibility for the others' children.

Although I have said *they know* these things, perhaps I should say that this is *how they feel*. Like the first generation born in a new country, they listen only half-comprehendingly to their parents' talk about the past. For as the children of pioneers had no access to the memories which could still move their parents to tears, the young today cannot share their parents' responses to events that deeply moved them in the past. But this is not all that separates the young from their elders. Watching, they can see that their elders are groping, that they are managing clumsily and often unsuccessfully the tasks imposed on them by the new conditions. They have no firsthand knowledge of the way their parents lived far across the seas, of how differently wood responded to tools, or land to hoe. They see that their elders are using means that are inappropriate, that their performance is poor, and the outcome very uncertain. The young do not know what must be done, but they feel that there must be a better way.

Just how they do feel was expressed in an essay by Shannon Dickson, a fifteen-year-old Texan boy:

> There is a mass confusion in the minds of my generation in trying to find a solution for ourselves and the world around us.
>
> We see the world as a huge rumble as it swiftly goes by with wars, poverty, prejudice, and the lack of understanding among people and nations.
>
> Then we stop and think: there must be a better way and we have to find it.
>
> We see the huge rat race of arguing people trying to beat their fellow man out. All of this builds up, causing unrest between nations and in the home. My generation is being used almost like a machine. We are to learn set standards, strive for better education so we can follow in our elders' footsteps. But why? If we are to be a generation of repetition, the situation will be worse. But how shall we change? We need a great deal of love for everyone, we need a universal understanding among people, we need to think of ourselves and to express our feelings, but that is not all. I have yet to discover what else we need, nor have I practiced these things as fully as I should. Because when I try I'm sneered at by my elders and those who do not hear, or look at it with a closed mind. Computers take the place of minds; electronics are taking over, only confusing things more.
>
> I admit we should follow some basic rules but first you should look at who is making the rules.
>
> Sometimes I walk down a deserted beach listening to the waves and birds and I hear them forever calling and forever crying and sometimes we feel that way but everyone goes on with his own little routines, afraid to stop and listen for fear of cracking their nutshell.
>
> The answer is out there somewhere. We need to search for it.

They feel that there must be a better way and that they must find it.

Today, nowhere in the world are there elders who know what the children know, no matter how remote and simple the societies are in which the children live. In the past there were always some elders who knew more than any children in terms of their experience of having grown up within a cultural system. Today there are none. It is not only that parents are no longer guides, but that there are no guides, whether one seeks them in one's own country or abroad. There are no elders who know what those who have been reared within the last twenty years know about the world into which they were born.

The elders are separated from them by the fact that they, too, are a strangely isolated generation. No generation has ever known, experienced, and incorporated such rapid changes, watched the sources of power, the means of communication, the definition of humanity, the limits of their explorable universe, the certainties of a known and limited world, the fundamental imperatives of life and death—all change before their eyes. They know more about change than any generation has ever known and so stand, over, against, and vastly alienated, from the young, who by the very nature of their position, have had to reject their elders' past.

Just as the early Americans had to teach themselves not to daydream of the past but concentrate on the present, and so in turn taught their children not to daydream but to act, so today's elders have to treat their own past as incommunicable, and teach their children, even in the midst of lamenting that it is so, not to ask, because they can never understand. We have to realize that no other generation will ever experience what we have experienced. In this sense we must recognize that we have no descendants, as our children have no forebears.

At this breaking point between two radically different and closely related groups, both are inevitably very lonely, as we face each other knowing that they will never experience what we have experienced, and that we can never experience what they have experienced.

The situation that has brought about this radical change will not occur again in any such drastic form in the foreseeable future. Once we have discovered that this planet is inhabited by only one human species this cannot be disavowed. The sense of responsibility for the existence of the entire living world, once laid upon our shoulders, will not be lifted. The young will hopefully be prepared to educate their own children for change. But just because this gap is unique, because nothing like it has ever occurred before, the elders are set apart from any previous generation and from the young.

This sense of distance, this feeling of lacking a living connection with members of the other generation, sometimes takes bizarre forms. In the summer of 1968 a group of American clergy who were meeting in Upsala talked with some of the young American conscientious objectors who had taken refuge in Sweden, and in a written report they said: "We are persuaded that these are our children." They could not take their cultural paternity for granted, but had to persuade themselves that it was so—after long discussion. So incredible it seemed—to believe that any of their children could leave the United States, where, in the past, the persecuted of Europe had taken refuge. They spoke almost as if a process of blood typing had had to be introduced to prove their spiritual paternity.

In most discussions of the generation gap, the alienation of the young is emphasized, while the alienation of their elders may be wholly overlooked. What the commentators forget is that true communication is a dialogue and that both parties to the dialogue lack a vocabulary.

We are familiar with the problems of communication between speakers of two languages who have been reared in radically different cultures, one, for example, in China and the other in the United States. Not only language, but also the incommensurability of their experience prevents them from understanding each other. Yet a willingness to learn the other's language and to explore the premises of both cultures can open the way to conversation. It can be done, but it is not often done.

The problem becomes more difficult, because it is more subtle, when speakers from two different cultures share what is regarded as a common tongue, such as English for Americans and Englishmen, Spanish for Spaniards and Latin Americans. Then true communication becomes possible only when both realize that they speak not one, but two languages in which the "same" words have divergent, sometimes radically different meanings. Then, if they are willing to listen and to ask, they can begin to talk and talk with delight.

This is also the problem of the two generations. Once the fact of a deep, new, unprecedented world-wide generation gap is firmly established, in the minds of both the young and the old, communication can be established again. But as long as any adult thinks that he, like the parents and teachers of old, can become introspective, invoke his own youth to understand the youth before him, then he is lost.

But this is what most elders are still doing. The fact that they delegate authority—that the father sends his sons away to school to learn new ideas and the older scientist sends his pupils to other laboratories to work on newer problems—changes nothing. It only means that parents and teachers are continuing to use the mechanisms of cofiguration characteristic of a world in which parents, having given up the right to teach their own children, expect their children to learn from other adults and their more knowledgeable age mates. Even in science, where we have tried to build in the expectation of discovery and innovations, students learn from old models, and normal young scientists work to fill in blank spaces in accepted paradigms. In today's accelerating rate of scientific discovery, the old are outmoded rapidly and replaced by near peers, but still within a framework of authority.

In the deepest sense, now as in the past, the elders are still in control. And partly because they are in control, they do not realize that the conditions for beginning a new dialogue with the young do not yet exist.

Ironically, it is often those who were, as teachers, very close to former generations of students, who now feel that the generation gap cannot be bridged and that their devotion to teaching has been betrayed by the young who cannot learn in the old ways.

From one point of view the situation in which we now find ourselves can be described as a crisis in faith, in which men, having lost their faith not only in religion but also in political ideology and in science, feel they have been deprived of every kind of security. I believe this crisis in faith can be attributed, at least in part, to the fact that there are now no elders who know more than the young themselves about what the young are experiencing. C. H. Waddington has hypothesized that one component of human evolution and the capacity for choice is the ability of the human child to accept on authority from elders the criteria for right and wrong. The acceptance of the distinction between right and wrong by the child is a consequence of his dependence on parental figures who are trusted, feared, and loved, who hold the child's very life in their hands. But today the elders can no longer present with certainty moral imperatives to the young.

True, in many parts of the world the parental generation still lives by a postfigurative set of values. From parents in such cultures children may learn that there have been unquestioned absolutes, and this learning may carry over into later experience as an expectation that absolute values can and should be reestablished. Nativistic cults, dogmatic religious and political movements flourish most vigorously at the point of recent breakdown of postfigurative cultures and least in those cultures in which orderly change is expected to occur within a set of stable values at higher levels of abstraction.

The older industrialized countries of the West have incorporated in their cultural assumptions the idea of change without revolution through the development of new social techniques to deal with the conditions brought about by economic change and technological advances. In these same countries, obsolescence tends to be treated as survival, loved or deprecated as the case may be. In England, the messenger who carried a dispatch case to France was retained long after the dispatches were sent by post; there, too, the pageantry of the throne exists side by side with the parliamentary government that has long superseded the throne as the source of power.

In Sweden the most modern laws about sex behavior coexist with the most uncompromising orthodox religious support of an absolute morality.

Similarly, in the United States there is both a deep commitment to developmental change, which is interpreted as progress, and a continuing resort to absolutism, which takes many forms. There are the religious sects and minor political groups, the principal appeal of which is their dogmatism with regard to right and wrong. There are the Utopian communities that have been a constant feature of our social, political, and intellectual development. And there is the tacit acceptance of a color caste system that exists in violation of our declared belief in the fundamental equality of all men.

Elsewhere in the world where change has been rapid, abrupt and often violent, where the idea of orderly processes of change has not taken hold, there is a continuing possibility of sudden eruptions that may take the form of revolutions and counterrevolutions—as in most Latin American countries—or may bring about, in sudden reversal—even though in a new form—the re-establishment of an archaic orthodoxy in which nonbelievers may be persecuted, tortured, and burned alive. The young people, today, who turn themselves into living torches mirror in very complex ways both the attitudes of orthodox absolutism and reactions to it. They follow the example of Buddhists who responded to the dogmatisms of communism and reactive anticommunism with an extreme violation of their own permissive and unabsolute religious values. But their acts also represent, implicitly, the treatment accorded heretics and nonbelievers by any absolutist system that allows no appeal from its dogmas.

There are still parents who answer a child's questions—why must I go to bed? or eat my vegetables? or stop sucking my thumb? or learn to read?—with simple assertions: Because it is *right* to do so, because *God* says so, or because *I* say so. These parents are preparing the way for the re-establishment of postfigurative elements in the culture. But these elements will be far more rigid and intractable than in the past because they must be defended in a world in which conflicting points of view, rather than orthodoxies, are prevalent and accessible.

Most parents, however, are too uncertain to assert old dogmatisms. They do not know how to teach these children who are so different from what they themselves once were, and most children are unable to learn from parents and elders they will never resemble. In the past, in the United States, the children of immigrant parents pleaded with them not to speak their foreign language in public and not to wear their outlandish, foreign clothes. They knew the burning shame of being, at the same time, unable to repudiate their parents and unable to accept simply and naturally their way of speaking and doing things. But in time they learned to find new teachers as guides, to model their behavior on that of more adapted age mates, and to slip in, unnoticed, among a group whose parents were more bearable.

Today the dissident young discover very rapidly that this solution is no longer possible. The breach between themselves and their parents also exists between their friends and their friends' parents and between their friends and their teachers. There are no bearable answers in the old books or in the brightly colored, superficially livened-up new textbooks they are asked to study.

Some look abroad for models. They are attracted by Camus, who, in his conflict between his Algerian birth and his intellectual allegiance to France, expressed some of the conflict they feel; but he is dead. They try to adapt to their own purposes the words of an aging Marxist, Marcuse, or the writings of the existentialists. They develop cultist attitudes of desperate admiration for the heroes of other young revolutionary groups. White students ally themselves with the black separatists. Black students attempt to restructure the past in their struggle to restructure the present.

These young dissidents realize the critical need for immediate world action on problems that affect the whole world. What they want is, in some way, to begin all over again. The idea of orderly, developmental change is lost for this generation of young, who cannot take over the past from their elders, but can only repudiate what their elders are doing now. The past for them is a colossal, unintelligible failure and the future may hold nothing but the destruction of the planet. Caught between the two, they are ready to make way for something new by a kind of social bulldozing—like the bulldozing in which every tree and feature of the landscape is destroyed to make way for a new community. Awareness of the reality of the crisis (which is, in fact, perceived most accurately not by the young, but by their discerning and prophetic elders) and the sense the young have that their elders do not understand the modern world, because they do not understand rebellion in which planned reformation of the present system is almost inconceivable.

Nevertheless those who have no power also have no routes to power except through those against whom they are rebelling. In the end, it was men who gave the vote to women; and it will be the House of Lords that votes to abolish the House of Lords, and those over eighteen who must agree if those under eighteen are to vote, as also, in the final analysis, nations will act to limit national sovereignty. Effective, rapid evolutionary change, in which no one is guillotined and no one is forced into exile, depends on the co-operation of a large number of those in power with the dispossessed who are seeking power. The innovating idea may come from others, but the initiative for successful action must come from those whose privileges, now regarded as obsolete, are about to be abolished.

There are those among the dissident young who recognize this. Significantly, they want their parents or those who represent their parents—deans and college presidents and editorial writers—to be on their side, to agree with them or at least to give them a blessing. Behind their demands is their hope that, even as they demonstrate against the college administration, the college president will come and talk with them—and bring his children. But there are also some who entertain no such hope.

I have spoken mainly about the most articulate young

people, those who want to drop out of the whole system and those who want to take the system apart and start over. But the feeling that nothing out of the past is meaningful and workable is very much more pervasive. Among the less articulate it is expressed in such things as the refusal to learn at school, cooperate at work, or follow normal political paths. Perhaps most noncompliance is of this passive kind. But the periodic massing of students behind their more active peers suggests that even passive noncompliance is highly inflammable.

Resistance among the young is also expressed by an essentially uninvolved and exploitative compliance with rules that are regarded as meaningless. Perhaps those who take this stand are the most frightening. Going through the forms by which men were educated for generations, but which no longer serve to educate those who accept them, can only teach students to regard all social systems in terms of exploitation.

But whatever stand they take, none of the young, neither the most idealistic nor the most cynical, is untouched by the sense that there are no adults anywhere in the world from whom they can learn what the next steps should be.

These, in brief, are the conditions of our time. These are the two generations—pioneers in a new era and their children, who have as yet to find a way of communicating about the world in which both live, though their perceptions of it are so different. No one knows what the next steps should be. Recognizing that this is so is, I submit, the beginning of an answer.

For I believe we are on the verge of developing a new kind of culture, one that is as much a departure in style from cofigurative cultures, as the institutionalization of cofiguration in orderly—and disorderly—change was a departure from the postfigurative style. I call this new style *prefigurative*, because in this new culture it will be the child—and not the parent and grandparent——that represents what is to come. Instead of the erect, white-haired elder who, in postfigurative cultures, stood for the past and the future in all their grandeur and continuity, the unborn child, already conceived but still in the womb, must become the symbol of what life will be like. This is a child whose sex and appearance and capabilities are unknown. This is a child who is a genius or suffers from some deep impairment, who will need imaginative, innovative, and dedicated adult care far beyond any we give today.

About the unborn child little can be known with certainty. We can tell with delicate instruments that supplement the ear that the child is alive, that its heart is beating. Other instruments, still more delicate, can give some clues as to the child's well-being. We can predict the approximate time when it will be born. We know that unless the mother is protected, nourished, and cared for, the child's chance for life will sink with her own; should she sicken and die, the child's life will also flicker out. But all else is promise.

No one can know in advance what the child will become—how swift his limbs will be, what will delight his eye, whether his tempo will be fast or slow, whether he will waken ready to cope with the world or only reach his best hours when the day people are tiring. No one can know how his mind will work—whether he will learn best from sight or sound or touch or movement. But knowing what we do not know and cannot predict, we can construct an environment in which a child, still unknown, can be safe and can grow and discover himself and the world.

In a safe and flexible environment there must be skilled care, anesthetics, oxygen, and blood on hand to protect the mother and the child in a difficult birth. There must be supportive care for the mother who becomes depressed or frightened. There must be artificial food for the infant who cannot be breast-fed. For the child who cannot sleep in the dark, there must be soft light. For the child who is sensitive to sound, there must be ways of muting noise.

As the child begins to reach out to people, he must be carried—held or propped or cradled—into company. As his eyes respond to color, there must be many colors, differing in hue, saturation, and brightness, for him to choose among. There must be many kinds of objects for him to classify, many rhythms and melodies to start him dancing. And as he begins to form an image of the world, he must have examples of the worlds other men have made and crayons and paints and clay so he can give form to the world of his own imagination.

Even so simple an enumeration of ways of meeting a child's needs makes us conscious of how much children have been bound to the ways of their forebears through love and dependence and trust. It also makes us conscious of how little flexibility there is in the child's dependence on adults as compared to the great flexibility that can be developed in the adult's succoring care. Without adult care, the infant will die in a few hours. Without adult care, the child will never learn to speak. Without the experience of trust, the child will never become a trusting member of society, who is able to love and care for others. The child is wholly dependent, and it is on this dependency that human culture has been built as, generation after generation for hundreds of thousands of years, adults have imposed on children, through their care for them, their vision of what life should be. Dependency has made conscience possible and, as both Julian Huxley and C. H. Waddington have argued so eloquently, ethics are not external to nature but are crucial to human evolution.

The continuity of culture and the incorporation of every innovation depended on the success of the postfigurative system by which the young were taught to replicate the lives of their ancestors. Then, as men learned to live in many different environments and as they traveled and traded with one another, contrasts among different postfigurative cultures began to provide the necessary conditions for change and for the development of cofigurative cultures in which people who had been reared to one form of commitment learned to adapt themselves to other forms but with the same absolute commitment.

Later, as the idea of change became embodied as a postfigurative element in many cultures, the young could learn from their elders that they should go beyond them—achieve more and do different things. But this beyond was always within the informed imagination of their elders; the son might be expected to cross the seas his father never crossed, study nuclear physics when his father had only an elementary school education, fly in the plane which his father watched from the ground. The peasant's son became a scholar; the poor man's son crossed the ocean his father had never seen; the teacher's son became a scientist.

Love and trust, based on dependency and answering care, made it possible for the individual who had been reared in one culture to move into another, transforming without destroying his earlier learning. It is seldom the first generation of voluntary immigrants and pioneers who cannot meet the demands of a new environment. Their previous learning carries them through. But unless they embody what is new postfiguratively, they cannot pass on to their children what they themselves had acquired through their own early training—the ability to learn from others the things their parents could not teach them.

Now, in a world in which there are no more knowledgeable others to whom parents can commit the children they themselves cannot teach, parents feel uncertain and helpless. Still believing that there should be answers, parents ask: How can we tell our children what is right? So some parents try to solve the problem by advising their children, very vaguely: You will have to figure that out for yourselves. And some parents ask: What are the others doing? But this resource of a cofigurative culture is becoming meaningless to parents who feel that the "others"—their children's age mates—are moving in ways that are unsafe for their own children to emulate and who find that they do not understand what their children figure out for themselves.

It is the adults who still believe that there is a safe and socially approved road to a kind of life they themselves have not experienced who react with the greatest anger and bitterness to the discovery that what they had hoped for no longer exists for their children. These are the parents, the trustees, the legislators, the columnists, and commentators who denounce most vocally what is happening in schools and colleges and universities in which they had placed their hopes for their children.

Today, as we are coming to understand better the circular processes through which culture is developed and transmitted, we recognize that man's most human characteristic is not his ability to learn, which he shares with many other species, but his ability to teach and store what others have developed and taught him. Learning, which is based on human dependency, is relatively simple. But human capacities for creating elaborate teachable systems, for understanding and utilizing the resources of the natural world, and for governing society and creating imaginary worlds, all these are very complex. In the past, men relied on the least elaborate part of the circular system, the dependent learning by children, for continuity of transmission and for the embodiment of the new. Now, with our greater understanding of the process, we must cultivate the most flexible and complex part of the system—the behavior of adults. We must, in fact, teach ourselves how to alter adult behavior so that we can give up postfigurative upbringing, with its tolerated cofigurative components, and discover prefigurative ways of teaching and learning that will keep the future open. We must create new models for adults who can teach their children not what to learn, but how to learn and not what they should be committed to, but the value of commitment.

Postfigurative cultures, which focused on the elders—those who had learned the most and were able to do the most with what they had learned—were essentially closed systems that continually replicated the past. We must now move toward the creation of open systems that focus on the future—and so on children, those whose capacities are least known and whose choices must be left open.

In doing this we explicitly recognize that the paths by which we came into the present can never be traversed again. The past is the road by which we have arrived where we are. Older forms of culture have provided us with the knowledge, the techniques, and the tools necessary for our contemporary civilization. Coming by different roads out of the past, all the peoples of the earth are now arriving in the new world community. No road into the present need be repudiated and no former way of life forgotten. But all these different pasts, our own and all others, must be treated as precursors.

It is significant how extremely difficult it has been even for the prophetic writers of science fiction to imagine and accept an unknown future. At the close of *Childhood's End*, Arthur Clarke wrote: "The stars are not for men."

Space operas picture the return of the last broken spaceship from imagined galactic societies to the "hall of the beginning" on Terra of Sol. In his *Midwich Cuckoos*, John Wyndham killed off the strange golden-eyed, perceptive children bred by earth women to visitors from outer space. The film, *2001: A Space Odyssey*, ended in failure. This deep unwillingness to have children go too far into the future suggests that the adult imagination, acting alone, remains fettered to the past.

So the freeing of men's imagination from the past depends, I believe, on the development of a new kind of communication with those who are most deeply involved with the future—the young who were born in the new world. That is, it depends on the direct participation of those who, up to now, have not had access to power and whose nature those in power cannot fully imagine. In the past, in cofigurational cultures, the elders were gradually cut off from limiting the future of their children. Now, as I see it, the development of prefigurational cultures will depend on the existence of a continuing dialogue in which the young, free to act on their own initiative, can lead their elders in the direction of the unknown. Then the older generation will have access to the new experiential knowledge, without which no meaningful plans can be made. It is only with the direct participation of the young, who have that knowledge, that we can build a viable future.

Instead of directing their rebellion toward the retrieval of a grandparental Utopian dream, as the Maoists seem to be doing with the young activists in China, we must learn together with the young how to take the next steps. Out of their new knowledge—new to the world and new to us—must come the questions to those who are already equipped by education and experience to search for answers.

Archibald Macleish wrote in *The Hamlet of A. Macleish,*

We have learned the answers, all the answers:
It is the question that we do not know.

His book was sent to me in 1928 while I was in the Admiralties, studying the Manus. At that time it seemed almost certain that the Manus, a people still proudly adapted to their stone-age culture, whose only experience of another kind of civilization was with the dehumanizing and degrading contact-culture, would eventually become poorly educated proletarians in a world they could neither understand nor influence.

Today, forty years later, the Manus people have skipped thousands of years and been able to take their destiny in their own hands, as they could not in the days when, locked within the stone age, they bullied and ravished the villages of their less aggressive neighbors. Today they are preparing their children for college, for law schools and medical schools, and transferring the leadership they once exercised, fitfully and with poor organization, in a tiny archipelago, as a tribe, into the wider world of a developing nation. And today, when the quotation came back to me, I phrased it differently because now we can say that we *do* know at least who must ask the questions if we, who have a long heritage of answers at our disposal, are to be able to answer them. The children, the young, must ask the questions that we would never think to ask, but enough trust must be re-established so that the elders will be permitted to work with them on the answers. As in a new country with makeshift shelters adapted hastily from out-of-date models, the children must be able to proclaim that they are cold and where the drafts are coming from; father is still the man who has the skill and the strength to cut down the tree to build a different kind of house.

During the last few years, I have been exposed to something that I at first branded as a temptation. Young people sometimes turn to me, when we have been co-operating vividly in a goal we share, and say, "You belong to us." This I felt to be a temptation which must be resisted at all costs, especially in a country where youth, in every form, is a tempting refuge for the middle-aged and aging. So I used to reply, "No, I do not belong to your generation. You think I do because you are currently in favor of things that I have been working on for forty years. But that does not make me a member of your generation. And how do I know that you will not in fact, be opposing these very goals ten years from now?" But I think that this reply was another example of our insistence that the future will be like the past, that most people go through cycles of revolt and reaction, that experience in the past can be applied to the future. Because I made that assumption I failed to see that perhaps they may have been saying something different. I was reared, as they wish they had been, by a grandmother and parents who did not think they could set their children's feet on any given path. I was reared almost seven decades ahead of my time, as today's twenty-year-olds proclaim they will rear their children, leaving them free to grow, straight and tall, into a future that must be left open and free. It is in a sense as a tribute to such a childhood that I am able to insist that we can change into a prefigurative culture, consciously, delightedly, and industriously, rearing unknown children for an unknown world.

But to do this we, the peoples of the world, must relocate the future. For the West the future has lain ahead of us, sometimes only a few hours ahead, sometimes a thousand years ahead, but always ahead, not here yet, beyond our reach. For many Oceanic peoples, the future lies behind, not before. For the Balinese the future is like an exposed but undeveloped film, slowly unrolling, while men stand and wait for what will be revealed. It is seen catching up with them, a figure of speech that we, too, use when we speak of hearing time's relentless footsteps behind us.

If we are to build a prefigurative culture in which the past is instrumental rather than coercive, we must change the location of the future. Here again we can take a cue from the young who seem to want instant Utopias. They say: The Future Is Now. This seems unreasonable and impetuous, and in some of the demands they make it is unrealizable in concrete detail; but here again, I think they give us the way to reshape our thinking. We must place the future, like the unborn child in the womb of a woman, within a community of men, women, and children, among us, already here, already to be nourished and succored and protected, already in need of things for which, if they are not prepared before it is born, it will be too late. So, as the young say, The Future Is Now.

APPENDIX A

Films, Slides, and Music
Used in the Man and Nature Lectures

When I gave the Man and Nature Lectures in March 1969, I used shot sequences from films, slides, and a music tape to supplement my own words. They are part of the record of what I wished to convey, but cannot include, except as references, in the published version.

LECTURE I *The Past—Postfigurative Cultures and Well-Known Forebears.*

BALIKCI, ASEN and QUENTIN BROWN. (Parts from) *Fishing at the Stone Weir*, The Netsilik Eskimo Film Series, Educational Services Inc., 16 mm., Parts I and II, color, 1966.

MEAD, MARGARET. *Four Families*, National Film Board of Canada, New York: Distributed by McGraw-Hill, 16 mm., black and white, sound, 1959 (Lullaby Sequences).

MEAD, MARGARET and GREGORY BATESON. *Bathing Babies in Three Cultures*, Character Formation in Different Cultures Series, New York University Film Library, 16 mm., black and white, sound, 1952 (Iatmul Sequence).

LECTURE II *The Present—Cofigurative Cultures and Familiar Peers.*

LOMAX, ALAN. Contrastive Styles in Adjoining Cultures: A Synthesis of Solo Songs from Manus, Ibiza, White and Black Spiritual Songs Sung by Mixed Choruses in Harmony, Lomax Recordings. Not for distribution.

Oss, Oss, Wee Oss. New York, Country Dance Society of America, 16 mm., color, sound, 1950.

Slides on Manus. Margaret Mead collection—hand painted and color, 1928, 1953, 1967.

LECTURE III   *The Future—Prefigurative Cultures and Unknown Children.*

BATESON, GREGORY. *Security* (Unpublished film of children's first experience with death), 16 mm., black and white, 1941.

CLAH, AL. *Intrepid Shadow,* Sol Worth and John Adair, producers, Philadelphia: Annenberg School of Communication, University of Pennsylvania; Part of series of seven films "Navajo Film Themselves," 16 mm., black and white, 1966.

——*Not Much to Do,* Privately made, 16 mm., black and white, sound, 1966.

APPENDIX B

Bibliographical Note

These lectures draw both on my field work in the years between 1925 and 1967 and on the work and insights of many of my seniors, colleagues, and students.

I have published extensive bibliographies on my own field work and the publications of others on the same peoples in "Social Organization of Manua," *Bernice P. Bishop Museum Bulletin,* 76 (Honolulu, 1930), in *Male and Female* (New York, Morrow, 1949; New York, Dell, 1968), and in *Continuities in Cultural Evolution* (New Haven, Yale University Press, 1964).

I have made partial acknowledgment of my intellectual indebtedness in the preface and the references cited in *Continuities in Cultural Evolution.* In *An Anthropologist at Work: Writings of Ruth Benedict* (Boston, Houghton Mifflin, 1959; 2nd edition, New York, Atherton, 1966), I have given a more detailed account of the early period at Columbia University when our first understanding was being formed of how culture is transmitted.

The selected set of essays *Anthropology: A Human Science* (Princeton, Van Nostrand, 1964) details in part the development of my understanding of cultural character and some of the measures I have thought must be taken in applying our growing understanding of culture to man's present precarious situation.

My understanding of the differential roles in the acculturative process played by grandparents, parents, and children developed slowly. I first discussed confusions of cofigurative cultures in "Education for Choice," Chapter 14 in *Coming of Age in Samoa* (New York, Morrow, 1928; New York, Dell,

1968). Shifts in sanctions and surrogates are discussed in "Social Change and Cultural Surrogates," *Journal of Educational Sociology,* 14 (1940, pp. 92–109), "Age Patterning in Personality Development," *American Journal of Orthopsychiatry,* 17 (1947, pp. 231–40), "The Implications of Culture Change for Personality Development," *American Journal of Orthopsychiatry,* 17 (1947, pp. 633–46), "On the Implications for Anthropology of the Gesell-Ilg Approach to Maturation," *American Anthropologist,* 49 (1947, pp. 69–77), "Character Formation and Diachronic Theory," in *Social Structure,* edited by Meyer Fortes (Oxford, Clarendon Press, 1949), "The Impact of Culture on Personality Development in the United States Today," unpublished address given at the Midcentury White House Conference on Children and Youth, Washington, D.C., December 6, 1950, and in *The School in American Culture* (Cambridge, Harvard University Press, 1951). *And Keep Your Powder Dry* (New York, Morrow, 1942; 2nd edition, 1965) spelled out some relations of immigration to character formation in the United States.

I first used the terms *prefigurative, cofigurative,* and *postfigurative* in "Cultural Determinants of Sexual Behavior," in *Sex and Internal Secretions,* 2 vols., 3rd edition, edited by W. C. Young (Baltimore, Williams and Wilkins, 1961). In "Towards More Vivid Utopias," *Science,* 126 (November 8, 1957, pp. 957–61), "Closing the Gap between Scientists and Others," *Daedalus* (Winter, 1959, pp. 139–46), and "The Future As the Basis for Establishing a Shared Culture," *Daedalus* (Winter, 1965, pp. 135–55), I began to develop the idea of the way the learning of children reinforms adults' understanding of their culture. *New Lives for Old: Cultural Transformation—Manus, 1928–1953* (New York, Morrow, 1956; New York, Dell, 1968) describes how one New Guinea people moved from the stone age into the present.

My first understanding of what was to come was expressed, I believe, in a poem I wrote in the 1920s *And Your Young Men Shall See Visions.*

"We have no past for fuel." The young men said.
"We have no long and dry array of husk-like hours,
  To bind in faggots, furbished for a pyre
  Where all our dead days blossom into flowers
  Of dream, renascent in the mighty fire."

"Cut then your future down!" The old men said.
  Fell the tall loveliness of unlived days;
  In such a smoke, new fathered of the green,
  Unsullied wood, in secret perilous ways,
  The unremembering young have visions seen."

NATURAL HISTORY PRESS BOOKS

ANTHROPOLOGY AND ARCHAEOLOGY

* AFRICA AND AFRICANS
  Paul Bohannan

** THE ARCHAEOLOGY OF MARTHA'S VINEYARD
  William H. Ritchie

** THE ARCHAEOLOGY OF MICHIGAN: A Guide to the Prehistory
  of the Great Lakes Region
  James E. Fitting

** THE ARCHAEOLOGY OF NEW YORK STATE (Revised Edition)
  William H. Ritchie

* BEYOND THE FRONTIER: Social Process and Cultural Change
  Edited by Paul Bohannan and Fred Plog

* COMPARATIVE POLITICAL SYSTEMS: Studies in the Politics of
  Pre-industrial Societies
  Edited by Ronald Cohen and John Middleton

* CULTURE AND COMMITMENT: A study of the Generation
  Gap
  Margaret Mead

* ENVIRONMENT AND CULTURAL BEHAVIOR: Ecological Studies
  in Cultural Anthropology
  Edited by Andrew P. Vayda

* EVOLUTION AND HUMAN BEHAVIOR
  Alexander Alland, Jr.

* Also available in a Natural History Press hardcover edition.
** Available in a hardcover edition only

* MYTH AND COSMOS: Readings in Mythology and Symbolism
Edited by John Middleton

NOMADS OF THE LONG BOW: The Siriono of Eastern Bolivia
Allan R. Holmberg

* PEOPLES AND CULTURES OF THE MIDDLE EAST: Volume 1
Depth and Diversity
Edited by Louise E. Sweet

* PEOPLES AND CULTURES OF THE MIDDLE EAST: Volume 2
Life in the Cities, Towns and Countryside
Edited by Louise E. Sweet

* PEOPLES AND CULTURES OF THE PACIFIC
Edited by Andrew P. Vayda

* PERSONALITIES AND CULTURE: Readings in Psychological
Anthropology
Edited by Robert Hunt

* TOOLS OF THE OLD AND NEW STONE AGE
Jacques Bordaz

* TRIBAL AND PEASANT ECONOMIES: Readings in Economic
Anthropology
Edited by George Dalton

* WAR: The Anthropology of Armed Conflict and Aggression
*Edited by Morton Fried, Marvin Harris, and Robert
Murphy*

** WAYWARD SERVANTS: The Two Worlds of the African
Pygmies
Colin Turnbull

THE WOODLAND INDIANS of the Western Great Lakes
Robert E. and Pat Ritzenthaler

ASTRONOMY

* DICTIONARY OF ASTRONOMICAL TERMS
Åke Wallenquist
Edited and translated by Sune Engelbrektson

* EXPLORATION OF THE MOON (revised Edition)
Franklyn M. Branley

** SPACE: The Story of Man's Greatest Feat of Exploration
Patrick Moore

BIOLOGY

** BIOLOGY: The Science of Life
Helena Curtis

* BIOLOGY OF BIRDS
Wesley E. Lanyon

** BLOOD
Leo Vroman

IDEAS IN EVOLUTION AND BEHAVIOR
John A. Moore, Editor

** IDEAS IN MODERN BIOLOGY
John A. Moore, Editor

** THE MARVELOUS ANIMALS: An Introduction to the Protozoa
Helena Curtis

* RAISING LABORATORY ANIMALS: A Handbook for Biological
and Behavioral Research
James Silvan

** RESEARCH METHODS IN PLANT SCIENCE
Richard M. and Deana T. Klein

** SEEING AND THE EYE: An Introduction to Vision
   G. Hugh Begbie

  * A SHORT HISTORY OF BIOLOGY
   Isaac Asimov

  * THE VIRUSES
   Helena Curtis

ECOLOGY

** DESIGN WITH NATURE
   Ian L. McHarg

** ENVIRONMENT: A Challenge to Modern Society
   Lynton K. Caldwell

  *ENVIRONMENT AND CULTURAL BEHAVIOR: Ecological Studies
   in Cultural Anthropology
   Edited by Andrew P. Vayda

** FUTURE ENVIRONMENTS OF NORTH AMERICA
   Edited by F. Fraser Darling and John P. Milton

** THE WOLF: The Ecology and Behavior of an Endangered
   Species
   L. David Mech

GEOLOGY

  * A GEOLOGIST'S VIEW OF CAPE COD
   Arthur N. Strahler

** THE GEOLOGY OF NEW YORK CITY AND ENVIRONS
   Christopher J. Schuberth

** A GUIDE TO THE NATIONAL PARKS: Their Landscape and
   Geology: Volume 1, the Western Parks
   William H. Matthews, III

** A GUIDE TO THE NATIONAL PARKS: Their Landscape and
Geology: Volume 2, the Eastern Parks
  William H. Matthews, III

** SOUTH OF YOSEMITE: Selected Writings of John Muir
  Edited and with an Introduction by Frederic Gunsky

** THESE FRAGILE OUTPOSTS: A Geological Look at Cape Cod,
Martha's Vineyard, and Nantucket
  Barbara Blau Chamberlain

NATURAL HISTORY

** THE ALIEN ANIMALS: The Story of Imported Wildlife
  George Laycock

** ANIMALS AND MEN: An Informal History of the Animal as
Prey, as Servant, as Companion
  Hermann Demback

** AUDUBON, BY HIMSELF
  Alice Ford

** BIRD MIGRATION
  Donald Griffin

** BIRDS AROUND THE WORLD: A Geographical Look at Evolution and Birds
  Dean Amadon

** BIRDS OF PARADISE AND BOWER BIRDS
  E. Thomas Gilliard

** THE BIRDS OF TIKAL
  Frank B. Smithe

** HANDBOOK OF NEW GUINEA BIRDS
  E. Thomas Gilliard and Austin L. Rand

** Island Life: A Natural History of the Islands of the World
Sherwin Carlquist

** The Last Paradises: On the Track of Rare Animals
Eugen Schuhmacher

** The Natural History of Dogs
Richard and Alice Fiennes

** The Outer Lands
Dorothy Sterling

Photographing Nature
David Linton

** The Sign of the Flying Goose: A Guide to the National
Wildlife Refuges
George Laycock

** So Excellent a Fishe: A Natural History of Sea Turtles
Archie Carr

** Wasp Farm
Howard Ensign Evans

** Wild Refuge
George Laycock

HISTORY AND PHILOSOPHY OF SCIENCE

** Bankers, Bones and Beetles: The First Century of The
American Museum of Natural History
Geoffrey Hellman

** The Coming of the Golden Age: A View of the End of
Progress
Gunther S. Stent

* THE IDENTITY OF MAN
  J. Bronowski

BOOKS FOR YOUNG READERS

** ANIMAL CAMOUFLAGE
  Dorothy Shuttlesworth

** ANIMALS AND THEIR WAYS: The Science of Animal Behavior
  J. D. Carthy

** BRAIN BOOSTERS
  David Webster

** CROSSWORD PUZZLERS
  David Webster

** THE CRUST OF THE EARTH: The Story of Geology
  Keith Clayton

** DESERT LIFE
  Ruth Kirk

** DISCOVERING NATURE INDOORS: A *Nature and Science* Guide
  to Investigations with Small Animals
  Laurence Pringle, editor

* DISCOVERING PLANTS: A *Nature and Science* Book of Experiments
  Richard M. Klein and Deana T. Klein

** DISCOVERING ROCKS AND MINERALS
  Roy A. Gallant and Christopher Schuberth

** ENERGY INTO POWER: The Story of Man and Machines
  E. G. Sterland

** EXPEDITIONS: Science Adventures from *Nature and Science* Magazine
Edited by Ruth McMullin

** EXPLORERS OF THE WORLD: Man's Conquest of Land, Sea, and Air
William R. Clark

** FALL IS HERE
Dorothy Sterling

** FROM GENERATION TO GENERATION: The Story of Reproduction
John Navarra, Joseph Weisberg, and Frank Mele

** INTO THE MAMMAL'S WORLD: Adventures from *Nature and Science* Magazine
Edited by Thomas G. Aylesworth

** IT WORKS LIKE THIS: A collection of Machines from *Nature and Science* Magazine
Edited by Thomas G. Aylesworth

** LIFE IN A DROP OF WATER
George I. Schwartz

** MAN AND HIS BODY: The Story of Physiology
Gordon McCulloch

** MAN AND INSECTS: Insect Allies and Enemies
L. H. Newman

** MAN PROBES THE UNIVERSE: The Story of Astronomy
Colin A. Ronan

** THE OUTER LANDS
Dorothy Sterling

** THE PELICANS
   George Laycock

** SNOW STUMPERS
   David Webster

** THROUGH THE MICROSCOPE: Science Probes an Unseen World
   M. D. Anderson

** TREASURES OF YESTERDAY: The Story of Archaeology
   Henry Garnett

** A VANISHING THUNDER
   Adrien Stoutenburg

** WORLD BENEATH THE OCEANS: Scientific Explorations of the Deep
   T. F. Gaskill

** ZOOS OF THE WORLD: The Story of Animals in Captivity
   James Fisher